CROSS-CULTURAL ESSENTIALS 2

GOD'S NARRATIVE CONTINUES: ACTS

A NEW IDENTITY IN CHRIST AND THE BIRTH OF THE CHURCH

26 TUTORIALS WITH DISCUSSION POINTS AND ACTIVITIES

ACCESSTRUTH

God's Narrative Continues: Acts
A new identity in Christ and the birth of the church
Biblical Foundations, Module 2 of the Cross-Cultural Essentials curriculum

Copyright © 2019, 2016 AccessTruth

Version 1.2

ISBN: 978-0-9944270-2-1

All Rights Reserved. Except as may be permitted by the Copyright Act, no part of this publication may be reproduced in any form or by any means without prior permission from the publisher. Requests for permission should be made to info@accesstruth.com

Unless otherwise indicated, all Scripture quotations are taken from the Holy Bible, New Living Translation, copyright © 1996, 2004. Used by permission of Tyndale House Publishers, Inc., Wheaton, Illinois 60189. All rights reserved.

Scripture quotations marked NCV are taken from the New Century Version®. Copyright © 2005 by Thomas Nelson. Used by permission. All rights reserved.

Published by AccessTruth
PO Box 8087
Baulkham Hills NSW 2153
Australia

Email: info@accesstruth.com
Web: accesstruth.com

Cover and interior design by Matthew Hillier
Edited by Simon Glover

Table of Contents

About the Cross-Cultural Essentials Curriculum 5

TUTORIAL 2.1 7
Looking through different eyes

TUTORIAL 2.2 13
Our Creator is always with us

TUTORIAL 2.3 19
We have a new, Righteous Representative

TUTORIAL 2.4 23
We have security because of the sacrifice of Christ

TUTORIAL 2.5 29
Jesus is our Passover Lamb

TUTORIAL 2.6 35
The Tabernacle reminds us of Jesus

TUTORIAL 2.7 41
God's Representative

TUTORIAL 2.8 47
God promised and then sent His Holy Spirit

TUTORIAL 2.9 53
God's Narrative continued - Acts

TUTORIAL 2.10 59
The arrival of the Holy Spirit

TUTORIAL 2.11 65
The meaning of Baptism

TUTORIAL 2.12 69
Life in the New Church at Jerusalem

TUTORIAL 2.13 75
God demonstrates His power through the Apostles

TUTORIAL 2.14 81
God guides the Church as they face challenges and persecution

TUTORIAL 2.15 87
Saul the persecutor becomes Saul the Apostle

TUTORIAL 2.16 93
The Lord sends Peter to teach the Gentiles

TUTORIAL 2.17 99
The Church moves outward

TUTORIAL 2.18 105
The Church sends out Paul and Barnabas

TUTORIAL 2.19 111
Paul's teaching journey continues

TUTORIAL 2.20 117
An important meeting and Paul revisits the new churches

TUTORIAL 2.21 123
The Holy Spirit guides Paul and his companions to Philippi

TUTORIAL 2.22 129
Paul continues visiting and teaching in the Aegean area

TUTORIAL 2.23 135
Paul teaches in Ephesus, with widespread results

TUTORIAL 2.24 141
God is with Paul as he ministers in Ephesus, Macedonia & Corinth

TUTORIAL 2.25 147
Paul is arrested in Jerusalem and imprisoned

TUTORIAL 2.26 153
Paul is taken to Rome and teaches there for two years

About the Cross-Cultural Essentials Curriculum

It's no secret that there are still millions of people in the world living in "unreached" or "least-reached" areas. If you look at the maps, the stats, and the lists of people group names, it's almost overwhelming. The people represented by those numbers can't find out about God, or who Jesus Christ is, or what He did for them because there's no Bible in their language or church in their area – they have *no access* to Truth.

So you could pack a suitcase and jump on a plane, but then what? How would you spend your first day? How would you start learning language? When would you tell them about Jesus? Where would you start? The truth is that a mature, grounded fellowship of God's children doesn't just "happen" in an unreached area or even in your neighborhood. When we speak the Truth, we need to have the confidence that it is still the same Truth when it gets through our hearer's language, culture and worldview grid.

The *Cross-Cultural Essentials* curriculum, made up of 10 individual modules, forms a comprehensive cross-cultural training course. Its main goal is to help equip believers to be effective in providing people access to God's Truth through evangelism and discipleship. The *Cross-Cultural Essentials* curriculum makes it easy to be better equipped for teaching the whole narrative of the Bible, for learning about culture and worldview and for planting a church and seeing it grow.

More information on the curriculum can be found at *accesstruth.com*

Introduction to Module 2: God's Narrative Continues: Acts

Module 2 starts by briefly looking back at the Biblical Narrative from Genesis to Christ from a totally new perspective: from the point of view of the identity change that has taken place for a believer. What does the Narrative say about their new identity, their access to God and their coming together with other believers? Module 2 also covers Acts, where God's Word describes the events that shape our understanding of our history as a Church, our shared identity, our mission, the Spirit's work, and the completion of God's Revelation in the New Testament.

ABOUT THE CROSS-CULTURAL ESSENTIALS CURRICULUM

How to use this module

 Read / watch / listen: Read through the tutorial. If you have an online account at *accesstruth.com*, or the DVD associated with this module you can watch the video or listen to the audio of the tutorial.

 Discussion Points: At the end of some tutorials there are discussion points. It may be helpful to write down your answers so you can process your thoughts. If you are doing the tutorials in a group, these points should prove helpful in guiding the discussion.

 Activities: Some tutorials have activities that involve practical tasks, worksheets that need to be completed, or may just ask for a written answer.

Primary Contributor

Paul Mac and his wife, Linda, spent 11 years in Papua New Guinea involved in pioneering church planting in an isolated people group. They were privileged to see God plant a number of churches in that area that continue to thrive today. During the time there, they headed up a translation team that produced a New Testament in the local language. After leaving PNG, Paul and Linda worked for 12 years in leadership and consultative roles with an international mission agency. Today they continue to provide church planting guidance for a number of different teams engaged in some of the world's most challenging contexts. They are passionate about seeing churches planted that are well equipped to carry on for future generations.

2.1 Looking through different eyes

✓ OBJECTIVES OF THIS TUTORIAL

We will look at the point in God's Narrative at which we have now arrived. Then we will introduce the next part of the journey, where we will explore where we have come from, and what we now have in Christ.

Introduction

Very shortly we'll continue with God's account - in the book we know as *Acts* or *Acts of the Apostles* - of what took place after His Son, Jesus Christ, the Messiah, returned to the realm where He always existed as part of the Three-in-One-God.

A hugely significant player in the ongoing Narrative will be the third person of that Divine Unity - the Spirit - His role as He comes into the world to live in and among those who believe in Jesus as their Saviour. We'll hear about some of the extraordinary things that happened to those who'd followed Him while He was on earth, and to those who became His followers over the next 50 or 60 years.

The Story describes how God continued to communicate with His people as He brought completion to His special Revelation, which He had written down by specially gifted individuals chosen by Him. Before we launch into that next chapter of God's story, we're first going to review some of the highlights from the part of the Narrative we've already covered. Because it is familiar territory, we'll move fairly quickly, and only stop here and there at significant landmarks. But the pace at which we go will not be the only difference. The perspective - the lens we look through - will be new in certain key aspects.

As we moved through the Narrative the first time, the whole flow was towards the coming of the Promised Deliverer. Our choice of what specific parts to cover and the things we focused on all built towards the arrival of God's Son in the world that He himself had created, a world that desperately needed the salvation He alone could provide.

Then, once He was on the scene, we observed how His life moved towards the climactic events of history - His arrest, execution, burial and resurrection. Everything in God's Narrative was drawing us on towards that great resolution of the terrible situation the world and its human inhabitants are in. What Jesus from Nazareth accomplished changed everything. From that point on nothing was, or ever will be, the same.

For us too, having followed the Narrative and then arriving at this point in the way we have, things should not be the same. Even if we were formerly very familiar with the Bible, hopefully this has brought into perspective again for us the incredible things God accomplished through the death and resurrection of Jesus His Son.

That's the amazing thing about the Good News that is at the heart of God's Story - the Bible tells us that it is a living, active and powerful force. Hearing truth communicated clearly - hopefully that's taken place here - should be a life-changing experience. For a new believer who's just accepted the Gospel by faith for the first time, the changes are obviously enormous. For those who've been God's children for longer, even if things are not quite so dramatic, the process of hearing God share His Story that culminates in the Gospel, should still have an impact... should still change our perspectives and help us see just a little bit more the way He sees things.

So, again, before we just steam ahead with the rest of the Narrative, we're going to take a brief time to enjoy looking back from this new perspective. Through the lens of what Jesus has achieved for us through His sacrifice.

Looking through different eyes

In many ways, the first time through the Narrative presents a very grim picture. On the whole, it is a story of rebellion, of separation, of pain and failure. The great Dilemma, the Problem, that man as a whole and individual people face in this world has strongly featured in the Story.

The results of Adam and Eve's sin jump out at us everywhere. God's Enemy Satan has usurped God's place and taken the human race captive through His deceit. Created in God's image and intended for a great purpose, men and women are incapable of fulfilling their intended destiny. They are cut off from God, with no way back. They are under His righteous judgment.

And this corresponds to what we see in daily life. It *is*, in many ways, a grim picture. There's just no way of getting around that. Of course in the Narrative, even at the initial dark moment of man's rebellion and fall, the small light of hope shone in the form of God's promise to send a Rescuer. And we saw that God continued to communicate. He provided a way for men to approach Him. But even there, we saw Cain's failure to come humbly in the right way, with terrible results. Things got so bad at one point in fact, that God even destroyed all but a tiny handful of the people on earth!

Of course, despite all this, God continued faithfully to move ahead with His plans to bring the Redeemer through a chosen line. He never gave up in His commitment to communicating with men, reaching out to them. His grace continued throughout as a shining strand of gold in the murky depths of human depravity and hopelessness.

And when Jesus, the light of the world, came, it was like dawn beginning to break. But it was really what He did by allowing himself to be crucified at Golgotha, and then what God did by accepting this payment for sin and bringing Him back to life, that finally broke the control that darkness had on the world. And for those who've recognized their absolute need and turned to Him in faith to save them, that light has illuminated their spirits and their lives.

So before we move on into new territory, we're going to take a quick look back at where we've come from…but this time with new eyes, as it were. Where before we kept coming back to the terrible situation the human race finds itself in before a holy God, now we're going to enjoy what it means to find ourselves forgiven by a holy God. Where before all the events in the narrative - the Flood, Isaac on the altar, the Israeli nation at the Red Sea - were powerful metaphors for us of the terrible situation humans without God are in, this time we'll see in those same events wonderful illustrations of what it means to be those whom God has rescued.

What it means to be safe

There's a moment in the early part of *Lord of the Rings*, when Frodo, Sam and the other hobbits are rescued from terrifying danger and brought to Rivendell. Frodo wakes up in bed, unsure of exactly where he is but glad to know he's safe. The passage says[1], "He lay a little while longer looking at patches of sunlight on the wall, and listening to the sound of a waterfall."

If God's Narrative has been clear to us, one thing we should know is that human beings on their own are in terrible danger. In fact, their fate is sealed. They live, often totally unaware, at the mercy of God's Enemy. Death is an ever-present reality of life. And death represents the end of any chance to know God or to avoid an eternity of separation from Him. Each of us has been in that situation, but God has made this clear to us. His revelation to people all through history - and to us, as we have been witnesses of His interaction - has been a cry of warning. As we become aware of our real situation, the appropriate response is fear… fear before a God whose holiness we can never live up

---

1. J. R. R. Tolkien, *Lord of the Rings: The Fellowship of the Ring*, Many Meetings

to. But as we've recognized that and put our faith in Jesus, God's perfect sacrifice who died in our place, He has forgiven us. That means we are now safe from His judgment.

Like Frodo, when he took that moment to luxuriate in the safety of a warm bed after being conscious of terrible danger and all the fear that goes along with it, let's take the opportunity to enjoy - and to understand a little more - what it means to be really safe. At that moment, Frodo didn't realize that before long he and his companions would set out on an epic quest. That, of course, is fiction, but God actually writes us into His Great - and real - Narrative. He calls us to be part of His Cause, His Rescue plan for the fallen race of His image-bearers. Before we learn more about that and, hopefully, embrace that Cause as our own, let's take a moment to gather our strength - or perhaps more accurately, allow God to give us strength - for what's ahead, by reviewing how He has related to His people in the past... reminding ourselves of all that He historically did for those who followed and served Him.

Different identities

There's another difference to note about our perspective now as we take a brief look back at where we've been. One of the really important themes in God's Narrative runs almost in the background and therefore often unnoticed - almost like a computer operating system - it is the whole issue of identity. Even though we've approached the Narrative ourselves for this first time as believers, we have not focused on our identity as His children. Because we were following the events more or less chronologically, we did not jump ahead to consider the implications of the Gospel in terms of who we, or who anyone else is. The identity of everyone before they've accepted the Gospel is dominated by our common ancestor, Adam. All the important things that came to characterize him after the Fall - rebellion, deception by Satan, suffering, death - also characterized us... the "us", that is, before we each repented and accepted by faith the salvation offered to us.

But now, having followed the Narrative to this point, we can enjoy looking through the lens of the Gospel - through the eyes we now have to see, because of what Jesus has done. Now we look back as the people we actually are, because instead of being characterized by and identified with Adam now, we're characterized and identified with Jesus Christ... and God says that He's pleased with, He's delighted by, He's fully satisfied in, His Son.

Transition to a new sector of the journey

Finally, there's something else very important to consider about the point we've reached. For much of the journey, we were covering the part of God's Narrative that we call the Old Testament - the large section of the Bible that takes its name from the initial covenant God made with His people the Israelites... defined by the Law He gave them. Then, when we got to the part where God's Son was born as human, we moved into the part of the Bible we call the New Testament - named for the second covenant that was instituted through Jesus' blood, His death. But the four accounts of Jesus' life - the Gospels - as a block, really form a transition between the two periods covered by those respective covenants or agreements. And the Gospel itself forms the actual pivotal point between the two great epochs of history. Now, as we start to hear the story of the first group of Jesus' followers, we're really moving into the second of those historical periods...all the realities and events of the past, present and future under the second of the great Covenants.

On an epic journey like this, it's worth taking stock of where we've come from, so we're prepared for where we are going. An illustration that has been used is of a long journey broken into two parts. The first has been overland, across mountains and plains. Then, having arrived at the shore, the travelers embark on a ship to complete their journey on the ocean. So that's where we are now, we're about to start on the second stage and we're reminding ourselves of all that has happened so that we're prepared for what's ahead in this challenging but exciting journey.

LOOKING THROUGH DIFFERENT EYES

❓ DISCUSSION POINTS

1. Describe in *narrative* rather than *propositional* terms what you understand the Gospel to be. Based on the Narrative so far (i.e. without quoting proof texts), reflect on what you feel it means when we say that the Gospel is powerful.

2. What has been your observation or personal experience of what typically happens to new believers in churches? Have you seen instances of a good plan being in place to take people where they are and help them on to maturity? Have you observed situations where pressure (intentionally or otherwise) is put on new believers to change their behavior… to begin to "act like a Christian"?

3. Picture yourself chatting with someone online who you haven't met in person. After a while they tell you they are a Christian. What do you say in response? How do you describe yourself? Do you ask them any questions to clarify what they mean when they say they are a "Christian"? If you would ask questions, what kinds of things would you be looking for in their answers?

2.2 Our Creator is always with us

> **OBJECTIVES OF THIS TUTORIAL**
>
> We look back at the events at the beginning of time, reflecting on God and how He revealed His character through His creative power, and enjoy our relationship with Our Creator.
> The portions of Scripture referred to in this tutorial are: **Deuteronomy 33:27, Psalm 95, Job 38:4-11, Genesis 1:1-2**

Last time
We thought about what we'll do before taking up the Narrative again and hearing what happens after Jesus returned to His Father in Heaven. We'll briefly review what we've already covered, but with some differences. Last time we were swept along by the flow of the Narrative as it moved towards Jesus coming to the earth, His life, then death and resurrection. Now we'll take a brief moment to look back at where we've come from, but through the 'lens' of the Gospel… enjoying the safety and wonderful new identity we have because of what He accomplished.

In the beginning…
As we go back to the very start of God's Story, we remember that it starts with those very simple but profound words, "In the beginning God…" (Genesis 1:1) In our society we're constantly assailed by all kinds of opinions, concepts, assumptions and theories that make claims to know how our universe began. The current three top 'hits' from a Google search for "origins of the universe" are entries from National Geographic, Wikipedia and Scientific American, all of which, not surprisingly, allow no place for the personal Creator God who states in the Bible that He was there "in the beginning".

This belief in the non-existence of God (and it is in almost every sense a religious *belief*) cannot by definition be based on any evidence. No matter how carefully cloaked in scientific language and theory, such assertions represent very clear commitments people make *not* to believe. For millions of people, when they look up into a night sky and imagine the vast expanse of the universe, they see only impersonal forces at play. They try to imagine a cosmos billions of years old…and God is absent from it. There's no one there to speak, no one to care, it's cold and still.

What a wonderful thing it is for us, His children, to think about eternity - or at least try to think about it - with God always there, always present. We find incredible joy and comfort in the certainty that we are not the product of eons of blind chance…or the eventual result of conditions created when an impersonal singularity in a black hole exploded matter into existence. When life seems to be spinning out of control and there's nothing to hold on to, when it seems like everything and everyone keeps changing around us… how amazing it is for us as God's children to know that He's always been there, has always been the same. In words recorded in Deuteronomy 33:27, Moses says to the Israelites - and this applies to us now too because of what Jesus has done for us - "The eternal God is your refuge and his everlasting arms are under you."

The Three-in-One-God

And the God who was there at the beginning, who IS there, is not just some detached impersonal force. The picture He gives us in His Narrative is not of some static existence, a kind of Divine singularity… like He's just 'there' in some purely mystical way. Not at all. God is alive in the fullest sense of the word, and more. And He's personal. Three persons in fact. The One-in-Three-God… Father, Son and Holy Spirit. Relating, communicating, unified as One.

The *unity in diversity* we see in the Trinity (having unique qualities but oneness in fundamental nature) will prove to be a pattern for what God wants to see among His people. Later, as we follow the ongoing Narrative, and as we glimpse what He intends for His people - how He draws them from the widest possible variety of situations, and makes them *one* - we'll see there a reflection of the Divine-variety-yet-Unity that existed even before the world was created… but that's still to come.

God created the universe

Then, God says at the beginning of His Narrative, He created the heavens and the earth. Although God was completely fulfilled, not needing anything to satisfy any lack, He chose to create the universe, the laws and reality that govern it, and this amazing planet we live on. Out of nothing, just because He chose to. He conceived the entire plan for this immensely complex and beautiful world completely from His wisdom and creativity… then carried out that plan through the power of His Word.

One of the much-loved songs of Israel, Psalm 95, calls them, and us, to sing and worship the Lord, the "Rock of our salvation", describing - metaphorically of course - how "He holds in His hands the depths of the earth and the mightiest mountains." It states that, "the sea belongs to him for He made it". And that "His hands formed the dry land". God, through these words of a song written by one of His servants, is laying claim to the world by the rights of Creator. And of course that's obviously the way it should be. He made it, and so He owns it. That too is incredibly encouraging for us. Even though, as we look around us today, it sometimes feels as if things in this world are out of control...although it might seem like evil is winning...that the darkness and chaos of the world system is dominating... we come back to the bedrock certainty that God, the Creator of the Universe, is the ultimate Owner. That's what we mean when we call Him Lord. He's the Master.

As humans, we tend to ask questions out of our very limited perspectives. But often we don't have enough basis of understanding to even frame the questions, much less answer them. This was the point God made when His servant Job questioned whether he'd been treated justly (Job 38:4-11). God responded with a series of His own questions, beginning with, "Where were you when I laid the foundations of the earth?" When we think about that it becomes laughable that we take it on ourselves to question the way God deals with us. He is God, the Architect and Builder of the Universe. He knew exactly where the earth needed to be in relationship to the sun to sustain life. And He knows exactly what is best for His children who He has ransomed with the blood of His Son, Jesus.

We know that after Jesus died He rose again and then returned in His new body to be with God the Father. This is related to His willingness to limit Himself - as a man - to a specific physical location. But God, as a Trinity, is everywhere at the same time. For those who are still under the sentence of God's judgment, that's a very scary reality. But for us who've accepted the amazing reality that Jesus took that judgment on Himself, it's a different story. For us there should be no fear at all in knowing that God is always with us, always understands what we're going through, always sees the things that we're struggling with. It means that He's always available for us to turn to and ask for His help, His guidance and encouragement.

God's Spirit created order and life

At the beginning of His Narrative, God describes the Spirit (Member of the Divine Unity or Trinity) as being there in a dark, chaotic and empty universe, ready to begin the process of creation (Genesis 1:1-2). In light of all the many ways people - including Christians - choose to understand this account, it's worth remembering that God chose to give this exact description, with precisely the level of detail He wanted us to have. His purpose for us as His children is to keep growing in our faith and appreciation of who He is in all His amazing majesty. He is in no way threatened by our questions or even doubts, but we have to bring them to Him honestly and humbly... acknowledging that they represent *our* lack of understanding, not a breakdown in His absolute power, holiness and love.

So the Spirit of God was there in the beginning with the Father and the Son, actively engaged in bringing light, order and life. We're reminded of the Spirit's work in our own lives. Separated from God, we were spiritually in darkness and chaos, and empty. But God's Spirit was there preparing our hearts for what only God could do. He spoke Truth into our hearts, shining His light and creating life where only death existed. And just like with the creation of the universe, He is committed to completing what He has started out on. He is devoted to the process of shaping us into the people He wants us to be. So we can relax in the confidence that we don't have to make ourselves better, to sort out the confusion that exists, to try to be different people. As we continue to listen with open hearts to His Narrative, He reveals Himself, His values and purposes to us… and His Spirit is eagerly waiting to help us apply those things in real life situations.

We read in the Creation account of each day unfolding, bringing new incredible things that God is doing. Everything is done well. Everything is excellent, perfect. That's who God is. He doesn't leave things half done. He doesn't start something and become bored with it. He gives himself wholeheartedly. He was making a place, a home, for His image-bearers. And He made a perfect fit between the home and the inhabitants. That provides us with another picture of what God is doing with us as individuals and - as His Narrative will go on to show - with us as a group (or *body*) of His children. As we know, God's Spirit actually lives in those people who by faith in Jesus, God's Son, have been restored to a relationship with God.

So the Spirit living in us will continue to faithfully work toward creating a place to live in that is according to God's design. Yes, we've got a long way to go. But thankfully we have the Father, the Son and the Spirit completely on our side. The God who designed then created the universe, including our amazingly complex and beautiful planet, is the same God whose Spirit lives in *us* His children… and who is committed to making the narrative of our lives part of His great Narrative.

? DISCUSSION POINTS

1. Reflect on the first sentence of Deuteronomy 33:27. What does it mean to you that the eternal God is your *refuge* (NLT) or *place of safety* (NCV)?" In your life, right now, do you feel that you often find your *refuge* in Him? If you were sharing these words from God's Word with a brand new believer, what areas do you think they would most likely need this applied to? How would you relate those thoughts to them in light of what they've already heard in the Narrative so far?

2. What do you feel is the right way to handle doubts or confusion we might have about God?

Should we:

a) Try to think of a verse or passage in the Bible to answer the question we have?

b) Ask someone else: friend, spouse, church leader, etc.?

c) View it as a sin that needs to be confessed?

d) Try to put the thought out of our minds?

e) Try to reason things out?

f) Bring the issue to God openly and ask Him to answer it somehow?

g) A combination of the above?

h) None of the above - some other way of dealing with it?

2.3 We have a new, Righteous Representative

 OBJECTIVES OF THIS TUTORIAL

This tutorial looks at the first Adam, in light of the second - the Lord Jesus Christ. When God looks at us, He sees our new righteous representative.
The portions of Scripture referred to in this tutorial are: **Genesis 1:27-28, 3:7,21, Matthew 28:18-20**

Last time

We looked back briefly at God's Account of the *beginning*. We reminded ourselves of how wonderful it is for us, His children, to know that our eternal Father has always existed, and that He made everything in the universe. Each part of the Trinity - Father, Son and Spirit - was involved in Creation, just as they are each involved in our lives. In the same way that creation was entirely initiated by God, saving us and making us into new people - a new creation - is something God planned and brought about. He's fully committed to seeing our lives become what He designed them to be.

Created for responsibility and authority

The Genesis account goes on to describe God's intention of creating a being that would bear the imprint of His - God's - own self. Because we are created, finite and dependent, for us, the desire to make something is always associated with some kind of need. But as we've noted a number of times, God's decision to create a race of beings to whom He could relate in a special way was not to fulfill anything He was lacking. He did not create a race of beings who could know Him, or who had the emotions to love, the will to obey and the capacity to worship Him, because He needed any of those things.

So this was an act of grace. To even exist, for us, is evidence of His grace - His kindness and favor that has nothing to do with merit. It's ridiculous to think that we might somehow *earn* the right to exist. But even more than this... not only did He create a specially favored race in His image, but He also gave them real responsibility and authority (Genesis 1:27-28). Built into what it is to be human He placed the capacity and potential to reproduce, to bring into the world others who bear the image of God. And He gave them - and through them, us - the enormous responsibility of managing the earth that He'd created. They and we were to be His representatives, directly responsible to Him, but with very real delegated authority.

Throughout the Old Testament Narrative we see many examples of God giving real responsibility and authority to His people. Then, as the Narrative continues, there's a lot of focus on how God's children under the New Covenant are given the ability and amazing privilege of being involved in His purposes. Clearly this is something extremely important to God, and another example of His grace. To be created in the image of God means that we're designed specifically to participate in what He's doing, what's important to Him. So when a human being focuses their thoughts, time and energy on something else, they're not fulfilling the very thing for which they were made. To state it in the positive: when someone is giving themselves to the purposes closest to God's heart, they are truly alive.

But of course, Adam and Eve were willingly deceived and aligned themselves with Satan who intends to overthrow God's rule. Now the race created by God to share with Him in His purposes had turned their backs on that privilege and - without fully realizing it - had aligned themselves with the Enemy, the Usurper.

Continuing to use God-given ingenuity down through history the human race has, of course, discovered and achieved a great deal. But without God's guidance and His purposes in focus, a lot of what man has done has also proved to be disastrous.

A new representative was chosen

Adam disqualified himself from the position God had appointed him to as caretaker over the created earth. His delegated authority was withdrawn. But God had no intention of allowing Satan a victory. The first representative of the human race had failed, a new one must be found. Someone who would be worthy to take the responsibility and bear authority in God's purposes.

At the moment when God was describing the terrible ramifications of Adam and Eve's sin, He also promised that someone would be sent to defeat Satan and restore man to the place God had intended for him. We know, of course, that in time He did come. And it was God's Son, born a human being, Jesus. He would be called *the Christ* - specially designated by God as His great Prophet, the final High Priest and the eternal King.

In the New Testament, one of God's designated storytellers, Paul, will call Jesus "*the second Adam*", the new man, the new head of God's family, representing His people before God. Unlike the first Adam, Jesus refused to listen to the Usurper. At enormous cost He put God's Purpose first and won the victory that had been promised in the dark day of the Fall. After Jesus bore our sin on the cross and then was raised back to life, He told His disciples that God had given Him all authority in heaven and earth. The first, only human, representative man, Adam, did have delegated authority on earth. But the authority of this second representative man, Jesus Christ, eclipses that completely. He has authority as God's Son in heaven and as God's appointed representative on earth.

We've already reflected on the fact that from the beginning God intended for His people to have the capacity and authority to be part of His Purposes. Jesus, the second Adam, made it possible again for God's people to fulfill the thing for which they were created. Immediately after asserting His authority, Jesus tells His disciples that they're to go out through the whole world telling people about Him and leading them to become His followers (Matthew 28:18-20). This is the great Rescue that Jesus came to the earth to initiate. And now, just before returning to God the Father in Heaven, He appoints - or *commissions* - His people under the new Covenant to join Him in this effort. Adam's role - and by extension ours - was originally to be caretakers of the earth. Now, Jesus' role - and by extension ours - is to share His great Narrative with people everywhere on the earth. The Narrative that culminates in the amazing News that on the cross, Jesus has solved the dilemma of sin and death.

Clothed in Christ's righteousness

The first time through the Narrative we noted how after their sin, Adam and Eve suddenly experienced shame. Where before it had not entered their minds to cover their bodies, they now felt exposed and guilty. Their relationship to the world around them, to each other, and most significantly to God, was now totally changed; corrupted (Genesis 3:7).

God rejected their pathetic efforts to cover themselves with leaves... only *He* could provide what would be satisfactory. Some of the animals they'd originally had under their supervision had to die. The Narrative says that God made clothes for Adam and Eve (Genesis 3:21). He provided the covering for the shame and guilt that had now come between Him and His image bearers. This provides a powerful metaphor for what God has done for us through Jesus' death. Every pathetic attempt of our own to deal with our guilt was doomed to fail... and only made it worse, in fact.

But God sent His Son who gladly died in our place. He took our guilt and shame on Himself. As an act of grace - we certainly can't do anything to earn this - God has covered us with the righteousness of Jesus.

When God looked at Adam and Eve, He could see the skins of the animals that died to temporarily hide their guilt. Now, when He looks at us, He sees the obedience, the perfection and the purity of His Son who He said pleased Him completely. And that won't ever change. The way He sees us now is entirely *in*dependent of what we have done, and, remarkably, anything we will do. His view of us doesn't change with how we feel.

We're going to highlight other places where the Narrative reinforces this incredible reality. And later, in the New Testament, we'll see that a lot of attention is given to this. One reason is because God knows that we are very quick to forget. The old habit of trying to find some way to deal with our guilt and our feelings of shame are very deeply ingrained. But He wants us to live in the freedom that comes from knowing that it has been completely and finally dealt with. We can live without guilt before Him because He always sees us in Christ… and that can never change.

? DISCUSSION POINTS

1. Reflect on what it means to you to have a delegated authority as a representative and witness of Jesus. How does that play out as you interact with people who are not believers? How do you see this authority you have from Him working alongside any other God-given authority in your life (e.g. your church)?

2. In your experience, do many Christians live with a clear sense of their guilt being completely dealt with by what Jesus accomplished at Calvary? Have you heard many people talk about, or much teaching about, the fact that we as believers are hidden in Christ's righteousness? What are some of the things you feel are the results of us truly understanding and living in the light of this?

2.4 We have security because of the sacrifice of Christ

 OBJECTIVES OF THIS TUTORIAL

This tutorial looks back at Noah and Abraham, and their lives of faith in God. We then see what their lives show us about our security in Christ, because of His sufficient sacrifice for us.
The portions of Scripture referred to in this tutorial are: **Genesis Chapters 6-12, 22, Luke 2:10**

Last time

We reviewed how, after creating Adam and Eve in *His image*, God gave them a position of real responsibility and authority. When they sinned, they - and we - lost the caretaker role over the earth. But God appointed a second man - Jesus - to represent the human race. Through His obedience and sacrifice, Jesus won the victory over God's Enemy and has been granted all authority in Heaven and earth. He delegates His authority to us, His children, to be His witnesses in the world.

We also remembered God covering Adam and Eve's nakedness with the skins of animals and were reminded that He has dealt with our guilt and shame once for all, by covering us in the righteousness of the Lord Jesus.

A way of escape for Noah and family

Ten generations, spanning a millennium or so, came and went after the Fall… with everyone born outside the special place, the garden, God had made for Adam and Eve. Each generation had passed on to the next their sin and innate rebellion against God. Each person was designed to bear the image of God, but was now marred and corrupted by sin. And each endured difficulties in life, pain, and eventually experienced physical death. Tragically, only a handful turned to God in faith and approached Him humbly in the way He had graciously given to them to come to Him as sinners. Eventually, broken hearted and sickened by the evil and corruption He saw in the race He'd made to bear

His image, God had had enough. He decided to destroy every human and all the other living things He'd originally given into the care of the human race.

Then, in God's Narrative we see one of the amazing instances when the word "but" is interjected, bearing great significance and hope. It's like the sign used in mathematical formulas for *doesn't equal to*. On one side is a scenario that all evidence and logic lead to hopelessness, impossibility, no solution. Then comes the word "*but*" or the phrase "*but God*", followed by some incredible act of His grace and wisdom that provides a solution only He is capable of.

The Narrative describes, on the one hand, the imminent and fully deserved destruction that is coming for every single person, without exception. But, breaking into that otherwise dark and grim picture we see God's grace shining like a beam of light. It picks out one man and his family, a man who is committed to knowing and following God, his Creator. He humbly approaches in the way God demands that sinful humans come to Him. He learns to walk in *close fellowship with God*, the text says (Genesis 6:9). God delights in this rare relationship with one of His image-bearers. This is what God created humans for in the first place. Yes, Noah is a sinner, a son of Adam, but God has established a way for people to relate on His terms, and by faith Noah has submitted to that. God is determined to preserve this relationship. He's under no obligation. Noah has absolutely no way of earning it. There's nothing God *needs* from Noah.

There's no light, as it were, emanating from Noah and his family, they are sinners like the rest, and deserving destruction. The light of God's grace always originates with Himself. But it finds those who turn to Him in faith and as God provides a way for them to be saved and to relate to Him, that light is reflected from them. So that's what happens here. God designs the ark to provide a way of escape for Noah, his family and representatives of each animal species. (Note the echo here of the caretaking responsibility and authority Adam had been given and then disqualified himself from. God's grace, yet again.) The rest of the population is warned, but they're dismissive, indifferent. The time comes; those to be saved are told to enter, the one door is shut tight. When the flood comes and God's judgment is raining down, Noah and his family are safe. It beats down from above and lifts the boat up from below. Those inside can hear it hammering above their heads, and feel the waves beneath their feet. But the devastation outside doesn't threaten them. They are protected by the means of rescue God provided. Safe in the warmth and light of God's grace when all around is chaos and destruction.

We are safe because of Jesus

This is a powerful picture of Jesus and the way of salvation that was provided for us. Hanging on the cross, He took our sins on Himself. We have believed in Him, accepted

Him as the only Way… the only Door through which we can escape from God's judgment that we deserve.

Then, like with the Ark, God's punishment poured down on Jesus. His terrible, righteous anger against our rebellion and sin beat down on His Son. But we, who actually deserve to be annihilated, are kept completely safe. God showed that His righteousness and justice had been completely satisfied by bringing Jesus back to life.

These are amazing and incredibly important things for us to understand, or at least *begin* to understand. We are safe. God doesn't want us to waste our time and obscure our relationship with Him now by agonising over this issue. His judgment for our sin *has* come, and it was borne by the Lord Jesus.

God's promises to Abraham

A few centuries after the great Flood humans were well on their way to repopulating the earth. God had scattered the people of the culture who'd attempted to build an enormous tower in the Babylonian plain in defiance of Him. Different extended family groups, now speaking their respective languages, were moving out in the global dispersion that has resulted in the complex ethnic picture we see today.

God had not forgotten His promise to send One who would break the hold Satan had over people. Despite the ongoing rebellion of the human race as a whole, God was committed to providing a way to bring them back into a permanent relationship with Himself. He had chosen a man, Abraham, to be the patriarch of a family line through which the Rescuer would come.

God made promises to Abraham about the future and instructed him to move with his family, eventually leading him to Canaan… this was to be the homeland of his family line, which would eventually become a nation. Later, after Abraham and his family were settled there, God renewed those promises. Understandably, Abraham was puzzled about how those things could happen, given that he and wife Sarah were by now past childbearing age.

These promises are among the most dramatic ever made to a man… through Abraham and the son that would be born to him and Sarah, God said He would bless all the families, or clans, of the earth. In other words, all the different people groups (Genesis 12:2-3). Some 2000 years later, when the ultimate fulfillment of those promises was born to a young virgin, Mary, an angel told some nearby shepherds that this wonderful event would *bring great joy to all people* (Luke 2:10). That has certainly been the case for you and I, and for millions of people down through history. The Saviour did come through Abraham's family line, exactly as God promised. We have been incredibly blessed.

So as we know, a son, Isaac, was born to Abraham and Sarah, exactly as God promised. And through him a nation was born. But much later, one of God's designated storytellers under the New Covenant will write to a group of Jesus' followers in the Roman province of Galatia - in modern day Turkey. He will make the point that Abraham also has a spiritual lineage which they, the Galatians, belonged to. And in fact, so do we, another 2000 years later. Because, Paul said, the real children of Abraham are those who put their faith in God… those who come to the point of no longer trusting in themselves and who put their faith in the Way that He provides - His Son, Abraham's descendant.

As we've noted before on our first time through the Narrative, God put His righteousness - His own absolutely perfect moral standing - to Abraham's account. Abraham didn't earn this in any way; it was an act of grace. But God did it when He saw that Abraham trusted Him for salvation. The same thing applies to us; God has declared us righteous because we've trusted Him for that provision. Today and forever, He states unequivocally that we stand without any stain of sin about us. Absolutely amazing, but absolutely true, because it is Jesus Christ who guarantees it.

Abraham is told to sacrifice Isaac

But before any of that began to unfold, Abraham's faith in God would, of course, be tested once more…and in the most dramatic way. God told Abraham to take his much loved son, Isaac, and sacrifice him as an offering. We know the story well. How they make the journey to the top of the mountain, Isaac carrying the firewood. How Isaac asks his father what they will sacrifice and Abraham's words - prophetic and full of faith - *God will provide* (Genesis 22:8). Then the moment of incredible drama… the young man bound, on the altar. The father, still believing implicitly in God who he's known and followed for so many years, about to plunge the knife down. And the command to stop at the last possible moment. A substitute is provided. In the nearby bush a ram, caught by the horns, put there by God to take the place of Isaac. What a wonderful picture God embedded for us in His Narrative, through this astonishing series of events! We know that like Isaac, we had no way out. Like his physical life, our eternal destinies were hanging in the balance.

We were completely helpless and unable, on our own, to avoid the inevitable consequences of our sin. But God, in mercy and grace, provided a replacement. The Lamb of God. The perfect substitute. The thing that had trapped us and made escape impossible - our own sin - now was put on Him. It was His obedience to the Father and His love for us that compelled Him to take our place.

❓ DISCUSSION POINTS

1. Imagine a friend - a new believer - who is concerned after hearing a well known preacher on TV insist that there's no way a person can know if they're saved or not… that we'll only know when God judges us after death. How will you try to help your friend if:

a) Their only knowledge of the Bible comes from studying God's Narrative with you up to the point we've now reached.

b) They have grown up in a church and heard lots of sermons and Bible studies at youth group over the years.

2.5 Jesus is our Passover Lamb

 OBJECTIVES OF THIS TUTORIAL

This tutorial looks back at the time when the Israelites were oppressed in Egypt, and with Moses leading them, God rescued them out of that oppression. In doing so, He gave us the picture of the Passover Lamb.
The Scripture referred to in this tutorial is: Exodus 3:13-14, Ch. 12, John 8:58, 1 Corinthians 5:7

Last time

We remembered that God providing a way of escape for Noah and his family from the Flood, was not something they deserved, not even because of Noah's faith…it was a measure of God's grace. When it came, the rain and floodwaters crashed all around but the people were safe and secure inside the ship that God designed and shut them into. This reminds us that having put our faith *in Christ* we are safe from God's judgment because it already came onto His Son. We also remembered Abraham's faith in the promises from God. We saw, in the story of the substitute God provided for Isaac, a picture of how Jesus was our substitute sacrifice, when we had no way of escaping the results of sin.

The Israelites are oppressed in Egypt

We pick up our brief overview of the Narrative four centuries, and some six generations later. Abraham's descendants now numbered in the hundreds of thousands. They were still living in Egypt after having moved there during the time Joseph enjoyed enormous status and authority. They had not assimilated into Egyptian culture but had retained their ethnic identity and religious distinctives, worshipers of Yahweh, the God of their forefathers. Wary of them as a potential military threat, and yet reliant on them economically as free labor, the Egyptian rulers instituted an official program of oppression. But how were the Israelites to think about God and the promises made to their patriarch Abraham, then repeated to Isaac and Jacob? Had God forgotten the promise to send One to rescue man? Would He perhaps not send Him through Abraham's family line? Had Yahweh abandoned them?

When we're facing really tough challenges, feel under pressure, or when we're being attacked by others without cause, we have to keep reminding ourselves that God is completely faithful. He doesn't change, He won't forget His promises, He's not at a loss what to do, and He never deserts us. If He didn't desert us when we were still His enemies as part of Adam's condemned line, what chance of Him doing so now that we're His children, ransomed by the blood of His much loved Son, Jesus?

God chose, equipped and sent Moses

Certainly God had not forgotten Abraham's descendants. And He wasn't indifferent at all to the things they were suffering. He would see that justice was done to those who oppressed His people. We can see a direct analogy with our own situation in God choosing someone through whom He'd work to free His people from bondage. In fact, there are a great many parallels that can be drawn between the life and work of Moses and that of Jesus.

To mention just a few: both were miraculously protected from death as babies; Moses was rejected initially by his people, and the nation of Israel turned their backs on Jesus; both performed miracles to authenticate their roles; both were used by God to free His people from bondage. This is yet another example of the way in which God, the Great Author, is writing His Narrative in real events, places and lives as part of His Revelation of Himself. This should be an exciting thought as we reflect on the fact that, as God's children, our lives too are a part of His Narrative... as we get to know Him more, align our values to His and allow His Spirit to guide us, we can actually contribute to His purpose of revealing Himself in the world.

An enormously significant event in Moses' life took place 40 years into his exile after running away from Egypt when he killed a man. It's another story that's familiar to most of us since Sunday School days - when God spoke to him from a bush that was burning but not consumed. During the ensuing conversation, Moses, insecure about whether he'd be accepted by his fellow Israelites as leader, asked who he should say had sent him. God gave His name as, "I AM" The only One who exists eternally independent of anyone or anything (Exodus 3:13-14). Only one other man in all of history could rightfully use that name for Himself, Jesus of Nazareth.

John records a conversation Jesus had with some Jewish religious leaders. He had just stated that their ancestor Abraham had been looking forward to His coming as the Messiah. When His audience questioned how Jesus, a relatively young man, could possibly know what Abraham had been thinking centuries before, He outraged them by saying that "Before Abraham was born, I AM." (John 8:58). He was asserting that He, like the Father, is eternally *there*, that He's *here*. Without need. Self-existent. Complete. Absolute. This is who our Master is... and He has said that He's always with us. *Because of Him*, and through the lives we now lead *with Him*, we have everything we can ever need.

Jesus is our Passover Lamb

We know what happened next. Moses eventually went and demanded, on God's behalf, that the king - the Pharaoh - of Egypt would let the Israelite people go. When he refused, God allowed a disastrous natural event to overtake Egypt. In the aftermath, the king said he'd let the Israelites go and worship their God outside the borders of his territory. But as the disaster receded he changed his mind. This pattern was repeated nine times, with the Egyptian areas being devastated while the Israelites were not affected... yet another illustration of how God always protects His own people and does not allow His righteous judgment to impact them. Eventually, the final act in this epic drama played out. Despite the Pharaoh's remarkably stubborn resistance against God, he was always destined to lose. God was going to take the life of every first-born child from every house, in a move that would finally convince the Egyptian monarch that he could not win. In his blind arrogance he had taken on the all-powerful Creator God, a most unwise thing to do!

As we know, God gave His people, the Israelites, a way to escape the tragedy that was about to overtake every Egyptian household. He gave very specific instructions about the lamb that was to be killed. God was again embedding in His Narrative an illustration, or *picture* of the Promised Redeemer.

Of all these *pictures* the Passover lamb is the most vivid. We'll remember of course that Jesus was crucified right around the time the Passover was being celebrated some 14 centuries later.

The early believers under the New Covenant would recognize this and, in fact, in one place Jesus is directly called *our Passover Lamb* (1 Corinthians 5:7). So God gave detailed instructions (Exodus 12). A lamb was to be carefully chosen by each Israelite household in Egypt. Not just any lamb but a really healthy, well formed, young, male. After being kept near the house for a few days to make sure it wasn't sick or failing, it would be killed at the designated time with its blood to be smeared on the door-frame. God, seeing in the blood evidence of death having already come and of that family's faith, would bypass them and protect them from the death that would otherwise have struck.

The parallels with Jesus, the true *Lamb of God*, are obvious, but nonetheless amazing. Still a young man at the point of His death, He had shown through His 33 years of obedience to God that He was the perfect sacrifice. At exactly the intended time, Jesus was crucified and His blood flowed out.

When we believed in Jesus' death, we entered into and so were permanently identified with that death, marked as it were by His blood… it's like we hide behind it for protection. So God sees that and because He's totally satisfied by His Son's sacrifice for us, He will never bring death to us. It simply cannot happen. Of course that doesn't mean we won't physically die. But instead of death being the start of eternal separation from Him with all its terrible implications, death for us means being with Him forever…being really alive.

God is our Rescuer

The events following the Passover are just as well known. But it's worth pushing through the Sunday School familiarity and even triviality that often gets attached to the stories and remind ourselves briefly just how dramatic it must have been. And also to mine the seams of truth God placed there to encourage and instruct His people down through the centuries. We thought last time about the powerful metaphors here.

The enormous group of Israelites were now on the move in the wilderness. But with their backs to the Sea and the king and his army bearing down they had no way of escape. How did they get into this situation? God makes it very clear in His Narrative that *He* had been leading them…visibly in fact, with a column of cloud during the day and fire at night. God's words to Moses make it very clear that He had brought the Israelites to this seemingly impossible situation to reveal something about Himself. He was going to show His glory and His power… to the Egyptians, to His people, the Israelites, to numerous others and to us, His children under the New Covenant.

There are some really important lessons for us to note here that should be both a challenge and an encouragement. Let's note a few:

- *God is always ultimately in control.* Even when things seem to be going totally wrong, and when we can't see His hand in a situation, we need to be confident that He is achieving His purposes.
- *God is always delighted to lead His people.* As great as it was for the Israelites to have something tangible in front of them, our situation is even better. We have the whole of God's Narrative, the example of Jesus, and His Spirit living in us to guide us.
- *God is more than able to deal with anyone who sets themselves against Him or who attacks His children.* We should be prepared to stand up for truth and for His name, but we do not have to defend ourselves or take justice into our own hands.

- *God never deserts His children, or leaves them to cope on their own.* And He always provides a way of escape. It might not be exactly what we picture being the best solution, but He will always produce an outcome that is for our best and that helps us and others know Him better. We know that God did exactly this for the Israelites. When all seemed lost, He opened up a way through the Sea. And then when they were safely through, He closed the water over the Egyptian army.

The Israelites were left praising God and expressing their gratitude to Him. We, His children today, have a great many things to thank Him for as well.

? DISCUSSION POINTS

1. In your own thinking how do you resolve the apparent contradiction between God creating us as humans with the freedom to make real choices and yet, on the other hand, Him orchestrating events and using people's lives to reveal Himself through His Narrative?

2. As we think about God calling Moses to a specific role and then his response, how does that relate to you and your experience? What degree of clarity do you feel you have right now about how God wants you to contribute to His purposes in the coming years? Are there major areas you currently see as limitations? What about your gifts and strengths?

2.6 The Tabernacle reminds us of Jesus

 OBJECTIVES OF THIS TUTORIAL

This tutorial looks back at the Tabernacle, viewing it through the lens of what we now have In Christ.
The portions of Scripture referred to in this tutorial are: **Exodus 20:1-17, Exodus Ch. 25 – 27**

Last time
We noted some parallels between the life of Moses and the life of Jesus. We also thought about how God gave His name as I AM to Moses and that Jesus also called Himself that to the Jewish leaders. Something else we highlighted were the parallels between God's instructions about the Passover lamb for the Israelites in Egypt, and Jesus, whose blood permanently protects us from God's judgment. And finally, we drew some encouragement and instruction for ourselves from the powerful picture of God intervening to rescue the Israelites at the Red Sea.

Only Jesus could fulfill the Law
After leading the Israelites out of Egypt and through the Red Sea, God guided them eventually to camp at the foot of Mount Sinai. We'll remember the proposed Covenant that He put before the Israelites there. The basic terms were straightforward. He would provide a Law, a constitution, if you like, that would define His absolutely holy standards for them as individuals and a community (Exodus 20:1-17).

If they could live up to that - if every one of them could fulfill it completely in every dimension of thought, word and action - then He promised they'd enjoy a special relationship with Him as a people. Their special relationship with the Creator God would be unique on the earth. They would have direct access to Him. He would protect them and help them to thrive as a people. We know the Israelites readily agreed, and just as quickly failed completely at keeping their side of the agreement.

But what about us? Do we have to try to keep God's Law under the conditions of the New Covenant? Do we have to earn God's protection and favor? Well for one thing, we have just as little chance of doing that through our own efforts as the Israelites did. It was realizing this reality that brought us to the point of finally giving up trying to please God ourselves and turning to Jesus.

Because the really amazing thing is that *He* did, and does, fulfill every aspect of God's Law…He lived, and lives, up to God's impossibly (for us) high standards. The New Covenant or Agreement or Testament - to use the old term - was made between God and His Son, Jesus Christ. Its conditions are upheld by Jesus' perfection and were sealed… or *signed*, in His blood. He paid the penalty already for all the times we have, and will continue to, fall short of His perfect standards.

As we've noted before, the mountain around which the Israelites were standing waiting for Moses to come down with God's Law, was shaking and smoking. God was graphically showing that He is holy and punishes sin. His anger against anything that falls short of His perfect standards is like a raging bush fire that vaporises everything in its path. The very safest place when there is a bushfire around is where it has already been… where there's no fuel left for it to burn. And that's where we are. By faith we've walked right into the place where God's hatred against sin has already burned the hottest - against His Son Jesus when He was the sin bearer. So because in God's view we're forever identified now with Jesus, we will never face that inferno ourselves.

The Tabernacle reminds us of Jesus

God, of course, was fully aware that the Israelites - as individuals and as a community - had no hope at all of keeping their side of the bargain. Despite that - another one of those '*but God*' examples of His grace - He was determined to relate to them and live with them as a community.

So He gave very specific instructions about a large portable structure, a very elaborate tent, in fact, that would be His special, holy place among them. As well as describing the layout, dimensions and materials to use, God also gave specific instructions about objects they should make as furnishings for this enclosed space.

For the Israelite community, those things served as practical equipment for the never-ending rituals needed to deal with their numerous violations of the Covenant. The furnishings were also designed to create a sense of awe at God's holiness and to highlight His *distance* from sinful humans. If we as New Covenant people could take a visit to the Tabernacle, it would be a very different experience than for the Israelites living under the requirements of the Old Covenant.

We can take a virtual tour in our imaginations:

The first thing we see as we enter the outer enclosure is a large **brass platform or altar**. A line of people is waiting nearby with animals to be sacrificed and burned there. Priests in their special robes are busy around the altar. We're immediately grateful that we don't have to constantly be bringing animals to be killed and burned so we can ask for forgiveness or favor. Jesus' sacrifice on our behalf completely satisfied God. We are totally forgiven. We can come to ask God for help any time, wherever we are. While we're grateful for the encouragement, fellowship and even guidance from fellow believers, we don't need to rely on other humans to help us approach God.

Moving on toward the large tent-like structure some meters away, we come to a **large basin** on a stand. This is kept full of water so the priests can wash their hands and feet before going into God's special place. Seeing this, we are reminded that God's Spirit uses His Word, His Narrative, rather like water to wash our hearts. In other words, as we learn more about Him and then ourselves in light of that, He helps us to align our perspectives, our values and our behavior to His. It's a process of cleaning away the old habits associated with our past identity and learning to live in light of who we are now… of allowing Him to shape us into what we are actually meant to be as His image-bearing children.

As we approach the Tabernacle, we're conscious that only the authorized priests from the line of Levi are entering…even into the outer room called the **Holy Place**. But for us New Covenant people, nothing is restricted and so we walk confidently on through the door. Inside we see a **table** that is completely covered in gold. On the table are **twelve loaves of bread** representing the twelve tribes of Israel. To us, the bread in this setting reminds us of Jesus who gives us life and strength. After all, He specifically said that He is the Bread of Life.

Over on the left is an elaborate golden object that has a stand on the ground coming up to **seven branches**. Each holds a burning **oil lamp**. Immediately we remember that Jesus said that He is the Light of the World. Because we know Him, we can live with real clarity and direction… we don't have to stumble around in darkness like so many in this world.

Since we came into the Holy Place we've been conscious of a really pleasant smell, and now we can see its source. Ahead is **another altar**, again made from wood but covered in gold; this one is smaller than the first one outside. On it we see **incense** burning as an offering to God. It makes us think about the fact that God is delighted by our worship, our prayers and our obedient actions as His children. Because we come *through His Son* - in fact, we regularly pray *in Jesus' name* - He finds them pleasing: a little like the way we appreciate something that smells really great.

Hanging at the end of the Holy Place ahead is a thick, colorful **curtain**, woven with images of powerful angels. We know that behind this is the room reserved for the shining glorious presence of the Almighty God. For those under the Old Covenant this formidable barrier was a symbol of fear and exclusion. Only the High Priest was allowed to go past this barrier, and only once a year after specific rituals and bringing blood. Anything else meant instantaneous death.

We, on the other hand, see nothing to fear there. To us it represents the body of the Lord Jesus which, while on earth, contained and hid the glory of God that is part of who He is. We are certainly sobered as we recall that His body was beaten and torn for us. But we're thrilled and thankful when we remember that moment just before He died when He said *It is finished!* and how the curtain hanging in the temple was torn from top to bottom.

And so, respectful and grateful, we walk in empty handed, without the need for any ritual, past the curtain into the **Holiest Place**. We can approach God's awesome Holy Presence with confidence…certainly not in ourselves, but because of Jesus' righteousness that protects us.

At first we're almost overcome by the brilliance of **God's Divine glorious presence,** but we remember that we live every day in His presence. Normally we're aware of His presence by faith rather than through our senses, but that doesn't mean He is less real, or less majestic. What an amazing thing it is to live in the presence of God and to have His Spirit living in us.

There's only one object in this room, a large wooden box or chest completely covered in gold. We know this is the **Ark of the Covenant** that contains the stone tablets engraved with the ten commandments. Thankfully we don't need to carry around something like that because God's Spirit is always with us, helping us to apply God's truth in everyday situations. The lid of the chest, the **mercy seat** is where the **High Priest** comes each year with lamb's blood to ask God to overlook the sin of the community.

As we stand there looking at these objects we're moved and overjoyed at the thought that Jesus is our High Priest. He is in Heaven, representing us to His Father on the basis of His blood that He offered as a sacrifice for our sins. We are completely forgiven. At any time of night or day, under any circumstance, we can come directly to God and be assured of His mercy and kindness to us. Our hearts are overwhelmed as we remember all the incredible privileges we have under the New Covenant that Jesus put into place for us.

? DISCUSSION POINTS

1. How would you answer someone who suggested that the God of the Old Testament seems much harsher and more vengeful than the loving, gracious God of the New Testament?

2. What do you think about the idea that as Christians we shouldn't really be worrying about the Old Testament? In your own words, describe how you think we should view this large part of God's Narrative? How should we interpret, or understand, what we find there?

3. If it's true that we do not need any particular rituals to worship God under the New Covenant, what importance do you feel we should place on church services? In terms of worship do you feel that church is:

   a) irrelevant,

   b) optional,

   c) helpful on occasions,

   d) very important,

   e) absolutely essential,

   f) something else.

   g) Please explain.

2.7 God's Representative

 OBJECTIVES OF THIS TUTORIAL

This tutorial looks back at the history prior to the birth of John. Then we look at Jesus' birth, baptism and temptation, and His life as God's Son and Representative on earth. What significance do all of these things have for us today?
The portions of Scripture referred to in this tutorial are: Luke 1:15,76, 4:14,18-19, John 1:32, Matthew 4:1

Last time

We remembered how God made a Covenant with the Israelite people. They were unable to even begin to live up to God's perfect standards as laid out in the Law. We gratefully reminded ourselves of the fact that under the New Covenant that we have entered into by faith, Christ has fulfilled God's requirements Himself and paid for our violations completely with His blood.

We then took a virtual tour through the tabernacle, noting what the different things there meant for the Israelites… and, in contrast, the amazing freedom, forgiveness and complete access we have to God as New Covenant people.

A brief overview of a millennium

In this brief overview of the Narrative we covered previously we don't have the time to linger on all the amazing things God has embedded in His Narrative that are a challenge and encouragement to His children… including for us who are in Christ under the New Covenant.

But to summarize: during that period, the Israelites who'd left Egypt - or rather their children's generation - did finally make it to the land that God had promised to Abraham. On the whole, the Israelites were victorious in the struggle for territorial supremacy with other people groups, but the threat of invasion continued for much of this period. In time, a monarchical dynasty was instituted, but only a handful of the kings over the centuries it lasted, truly followed the Creator God. After the death of the third king, Solomon (who constructed the temple in Jerusalem), the nation divided into north and south kingdoms. Despite numerous warnings from God through His prophets, the majority of the rulers and their people - in both kingdoms - continued to be drawn into the polytheism and cultic practices of neighboring ethnic groups.

Eventually God used two of the regional super-powers of the time, Babylon and Assyria, to bring His judgment on the respective Israeli kingdoms through devastating military defeats and mass captivity. On their return in the 6th century before Christ, they rebuilt the temple that had been destroyed in the invasions. The temple would later be greatly expanded and virtually rebuilt by King Herod. For 400 years God did not add to His Narrative through the prophets. During this time Greek culture spread throughout the Mediterranean basin and beyond, soon to be followed by the Roman Empire. Israel was invaded and occupied by Rome. The scene was set for the arrival of Jesus, the fulfillment of so many promises and prophecies.

John, the messenger

Just like with Creation, the Incarnation - God the Father sending His Son into the world as a human - took place with a high level of involvement by God's Spirit. We see this first in the events leading up to the arrival, and then in the life, of John... the one who would be known for challenging the Jews about their sin, and then helping them demonstrate their repentance through baptism. Luke records the pronouncement of one of God's messenger angels who said that John would be controlled by God's Holy Spirit right from his birth (Luke 1:15).

God's Spirit had a significant role throughout the entire first Covenant period. He was the one who gave special abilities for certain tasks such as the construction of the tabernacle and temple. He was also the one who guided God's designated storytellers - His *prophets* - with the insights and the words they would record in the written Narrative. But from this point on, and certainly following Jesus' return to the Father after His resurrection, the Spirit would increasingly feature in the Narrative.

At John's birth, his father Zacharias was given special ability by God's Spirit to foresee what would shape his son's life. He announced that John was to have the unique privilege of proclaiming God's truth in order to prepare people for the coming Messiah (Luke 1:76).

Jesus' relationship with the Father and Holy Spirit

The way that God's Son became a human being was a miracle that God's Spirit Himself brought about. In an event wrapped in mystery to our limited minds and far beyond the narrow sphere of science, the Creator and Sustainer of life became a human embryo in the womb of a virgin. This life of the promised Saviour was mothered *naturally* by Mary, a young woman of the first century from the town of Nazareth…but fathered *supernaturally* by the eternal God of Heaven.

As close relatives, and with only six months difference in age, the young John and Jesus may well have spent time together…the Narrative doesn't say. There's actually only one recorded encounter, but it is a highly significant one. One day, among the group of people coming to be baptized in the Jordan, John was startled to see his cousin, Jesus. John knew by this stage that this was the long-promised Messiah, and he says that it would be much more appropriate for Jesus to baptize *him*. But Jesus insisted. Even though He had nothing for which to repent, by being baptized, He demonstrated His obedience before God. He also associated Himself with the common people, with *us* in fact.

His baptism was also full of important symbolism related to what was ahead. In going down under the water, Jesus was portraying the death and burial that He would go through as our representative. Then, coming up out of the water was a picture of His resurrection that would bring new life to everyone who, like us, believes in Him.

Everything was now ready for Jesus to launch into the next three years that would prove to be so important, and which would end in His death. But He wouldn't launch into all that on His own… He was committed to being reliant on God for everything He needed. And He was given God's full support. First of all, a complete endorsement from His Father who announced that this was His Son who He was completely pleased with. Then the Spirit, represented in the physical world by a dove-like shape, came down from heaven to "rest on Jesus" as the text describes it (John 1:32). What God was indicating was that His Spirit would be with Jesus to give Him the resources He needed to do everything the Father asked of Him. He would live with Him, not to "possess" and annihilate His personhood in the way the evil spirits love to do, but to be there. This was different to the kind of limited assistance given by the Spirit to individuals for a specific task as we see in the Narrative of the First Covenant. Jesus would have constant access to God's power and wisdom through His Spirit. As we'll see in the ongoing Narrative, this is exactly the kind of relationship we have with God. Jesus paved the way, and modeled for us, how God wants to relate to us as His children. His complete approval of Jesus applies fully to us. The Spirit also comes and lives permanently with us to give us all the resources we need to live as the Father wants us to, and to do the work He gives us.

The relationship tested

As we noted before, this close relationship with God was immediately probed for weak spots or flaw lines… could Jesus be tempted to place a higher value on anything over the relationship with His Father and the Holy Spirit? God's Spirit leads Jesus into the uninhabited, desert wasteland to face God's Enemy. (Matthew 4:1)

Thousands of years before, Satan had tested Adam and Eve in a similar way and found, to his great satisfaction and their great loss, that they were willing to forego their relationship with God for a sense (a false one as it turned out) of self-determination and freedom. Would Jesus fall for this as well? We know that He did not. Each time, as God's Enemy looked for a point of vulnerability, Jesus relied, not on His own eloquence or cleverness, but on God's wisdom already accessible in His Narrative. The thing He wanted to know and then apply to whatever area He was being tested in, was *what God has said*...what had God revealed about Himself that was relevant to the situation and how could He apply it to this real-life situation? Which - as other parts of His Narrative describe - forms the *armor* and *ammunition* that is available to *us* to handle similar attacks.

The candidate for representative of the human race before God had proved Himself worthy. At that initial trial, and with every single thing He did and said over the next three years He would demonstrate beyond a shadow of doubt that He was entirely different from the first representative, Adam. So for us who are under Jesus' leadership, Satan no longer has authority over us. Our Representative has triumphed and *in Him* so do we!

Jesus begins His work in earnest

Having received God's complete endorsement and with His Spirit providing guidance and resources...and having proved Himself worthy in the face of Satan's attack, Jesus launched head on into the Task He had come for. Luke tells us that Jesus now returned to His home area of Galilee, "filled with the Holy Spirit's power" (Luke 4:14). He started traveling around to local towns, going to the synagogues and showing how God's Narrative - only the First Covenant part was completed then, of course - all pointed towards Him.

Luke describes an occasion one Saturday - the Sabbath - when Jesus was in the synagogue of His home town of Nazareth. He chose a passage written by God's prophet Isaiah that everyone present would have known was talking about the Messiah...what we now identity as verses 18 and 19 of chapter 4. Most likely He was reading in the original Hebrew, words the New Living Translation (NLT) expresses in English like this, "*The Spirit of the Lord is upon me, for He has anointed me to bring Good News to the poor. He has sent me to proclaim that captives will be released, that the blind will see, that the oppressed will be set free, and that the time of the Lord's favor has come.*"

As we look back from our vantage point we can appreciate the far-reaching implications of these words much more fully even than those people from His home town. God most definitely cares deeply about the physical and emotional pain human beings experience in this fallen, corrupted world. In fact, in the coming weeks and months, Jesus would circumvent so-called 'natural' laws to alleviate pain and suffering for many needy people He encountered. But as the Narrative unfolds it becomes obvious that these miracles are motivated by a concern that goes well beyond their immediate *felt*, and even *real* needs. He used those miraculous signs to demonstrate His power as God's Son because He wanted them to see Him as the Cure for the thing that really ailed them. Every problem, disadvantage, handicap, obstacle or injustice people can legitimately point to is overshadowed by their one really big dilemma... their need to be made right before a perfect, holy, righteous God.

So when we hear those words Jesus read to the people in His home town, they resonate deeply with us. In the ways that really matter - in dimensions that extend beyond this physical world - we are beggars who've inherited enormous wealth; death-row prisoners breathing the free air; people blind from birth now luxuriating in sight; members of a tyrannized class getting used to acceptance and honor. That's what Jesus was telling those people from His home town that God's Spirit was giving Him the ability and authority to achieve. Of course as we know, they rejected Him and His message, as did most of His countrymen.

? DISCUSSION POINTS

1. In your own words, what do you think it means when God's Word says that Jesus was "filled with the Holy Spirit's power"? Do you think there was any time when Jesus was more or less filled with the Holy Spirit than another? Please explain.

2. If a friend who claims to be a Christian said to you that they don't really feel free - that they've always had a sense of being restricted and weighed down in their faith - what would you say to them? How would you express how you feel about freedom and liberty as God's child?

2.8 God promised & then sent His Holy Spirit

 OBJECTIVES OF THIS TUTORIAL

This tutorial looks again at the time when Jesus left the earth to go to the place where we also will go. It discusses the coming of the Holy Spirit, His role at that time, and how He is helping us today.
The Scripture referred to in this tutorial is: Mark 14:22-24, John 14:1-3,15-17,26, 16:12-15, Acts 1:4,8

Last time

We moved quickly past 1000 years of history to John, who was given the task of preparing people for the Messiah's arrival. God's Spirit equipped John for the work he had to do. After John baptized Jesus and God announced that He was completely pleased with His Son, God's Spirit came to stay with Him 24/7 so He could give Jesus the wisdom and power from God He'd need for everything. Satan immediately tested His special relationship with God, but Jesus was unmoved in His commitment to being guided by God's Word and Spirit. Jesus began to use God's Narrative to declare who He was to His own people.

Jesus shared a final meal with His disciples

As we know, Jesus chose twelve men to be His close followers during the time He was traveling around and teaching. While they were with Him He was preparing them to be His appointed witnesses and representatives - *Apostles* is the specific term used. He modeled for them how to share God's Narrative with others in such a way that people would understand and accept the Good News about Him... they were also learning invaluable lessons about what to teach and how to disciple any who did accept that Good News. And we know that of those twelve, only one - Judas - failed to go on and give their lives for the Task Jesus equipped them for.

But let's fast-forward about three years. Jesus' disciples had seen and heard some amazing things during that period. He had healed many people of sickness, caused blind people to see again, made legs and arms deformed from birth function normally, even brought people back to life...He'd calmed storms, fed thousands with just a few fragments of food, and ordered demons out of many people who they'd been tormenting. He'd also taught many people in their town synagogues, at the Temple in Jerusalem, beside roads and the lake in Galilee and on hilltops. He'd challenged assumptions, put His finger on areas of spiritual ignorance, and exposed hypocrisy - particularly among the Jewish religious leaders. The Jewish leaders had grown to hate Him for it. They were jealous because of the crowds that He was drawing. They were afraid that the occupying Romans would use it as an excuse to clamp down and reduce their powers... they'd lose their power over their fellow Jews with all the associated lifestyle benefits.

Things were coming to a head. Jerusalem was crowded with Jews from all over the Mediterranean basin, there for the Passover festival. Judas Iscariot had conspired with the Jewish leaders to betray Jesus to them. Jesus knew all of this of course...knew that He had only a short time left with His disciples before His death. He and His disciples found a place to eat the Passover meal together. This was the most important festival related to the Old Covenant. It reminded them of God's mercy and protection on that one night in Egypt, but also of the escape from slavery and the special relationship God had with His chosen people.

Now Jesus introduced something that would replace the Passover with a way for *us* under the New Covenant to remember God's grace and mercy. A simple way to regularly remind ourselves what it cost Jesus to rescue *us* from spiritual bondage... also to celebrate the relationship we have together with Him, and to look forward with joy to being with Him forever.

We're familiar with the simple symbols...He used bread because that was on the table in front of Him. He told the disciples that just as He was breaking it and handing it around to them, His body would be injured as a sacrifice for the sins of others. Then, He picked up a cup of wine and said that it represented His blood that would run out in the process of Him being sacrificed. *He* was the final and ultimate Passover lamb. *His* blood satisfied God's righteous demands for justice against sin (Mark 14:22-24).

And so, as He explained, His blood would confirm a New Covenant between God and His people...all the old, inadequate rituals and measures for covering people's sin, getting them through another day, another month and year, avoiding God's judgment, hoping they'd done what was needed for His favor... all of that was to be done away with. So now, when a group of us under the New Covenant remember Him in a similar way to how He and His disciples did that night, it's definitely not a ritual that changes anything in God's eyes. Nothing magical happens, it's just a simple bit of food we eat and liquid we drink. But we do it because our Lord said He wants us to, and because it is a wonderful way for us to regularly remember what He did for us.

All this talk about Him dying and leaving was confusing and distressing for the disciples. Why did He have to die? Where was He going? And where would that leave them and His other followers... a small group of mostly uneducated, politically powerless people? How would they know what to do? Who would encourage them? What hope would there be of the Good News about Him spreading?

Jesus is already there - where we are going

Jesus knew everything that was bothering them, including their unspoken questions... just as He knows ours. He told them that their future was bright and full of hope (John 14:1-3). Yes, He was going away, but the parting would only be temporary. In time, they'd be reunited in a place that He was going to get ready for them. And at that point, it would be permanent... they'd always be with Him from then on.

What was true for those rather sad, confused men with Him that night is true for us. When we're confused and discouraged, this is something amazing we have to hold on to... a certainty we can look forward to. When Jesus died He rose again with a different kind of body, one that cannot die... but a real body nonetheless. The disciples could see and talk with Him. He ate food with them. One of them, Thomas, was able to put his hand on Jesus' side where He'd been wounded. The point is, when Jesus left the earth to return to His Father, He went to a real place. We can't really understand *where* that is. It won't show up on a GPS search or on Google Maps, but it's real... in fact, more 'real' than the places we know that actually won't last forever. Jesus has gone there before us and is eagerly waiting for the time when we'll join Him.

He promised to send God's Spirit to guide them

But as real and encouraging as that might be, it's in the future. What about now? How would the disciples survive in a culture that was, on the whole, antagonistic to Jesus and those who follow Him? How would they know how to live, and how to relate to others?

Jesus had the solution ready before they'd even begun to form the questions in their minds. He said He'd send someone else to fill the need they were sensing. The term He used for this person was the Greek word *paráklētos*, which has been translated into English as Comforter, Helper, and also Advocate (John 14:15-17, 26). All these shades of meaning are most definitely true of the One He was sending. Jesus explained that He was talking about God's Holy Spirit... the One who had been present at Creation, who'd given people the wisdom and strength for specific tasks during Old Covenant times, and who had been with Jesus the whole time He'd been teaching and doing miracles.

So yes, Jesus was leaving them in a physical sense, but God would send His Spirit to take His place and do everything - and more - that they'd been relying on Jesus for. The distinguishing characteristic of the Spirit He highlighted was that He *leads into all truth*. What He'd be putting His limitless energy into once He had come to live in them would be helping them know, understand, believe in and live out, the *Truth. All truth*... the whole of God's Narrative. In fact, some of those men who were there would be given the special privilege of adding to God's written Word. They had the Narrative from the Old Covenant, and now guided by the Spirit they would soon begin writing the final chapters - God's Narrative for the New Covenant. But they, themselves, would also be part of what God was revealing to the world. The Spirit would lead them to align their lives to the truth...the Truth that they'd been eyewitnesses to as they'd been with Jesus for the last three years.

The Spirit would also give them the ability to communicate that truth with individuals and communities trapped by Satan's lies and the false narratives that they've told themselves.

The disciples didn't need to be concerned that they'd forget the things Jesus had said... He reassured them that the Holy Spirit would constantly remind them of *everything* they had learned from Him. Actually, as things stood at that moment, there were many areas the disciples wouldn't be able to understand. But the Spirit would come and build on the truth-foundations Jesus had already laid (John 16:12-15). He would do His work with care and precision, gradually helping them understand all the Narrative threads - past and future - that tie together in Jesus Christ. The incredible thing for us is that the Holy Spirit also lives in us and is helping us to understand Truth in the same way Jesus promised.

The Spirit would equip them for the Task

The disciples would experience a roller coaster of emotions in the days after Jesus told them these things. The fear and confusion of His arrest, the trauma and devastation of His death, then the jubilant excitement of finding out that He was alive again. They had spent some time with Him, but must have sensed that things were not like before. It was not going to go on like this indefinitely.

Forty days after His resurrection they were gathered together with Him again... minus Judas Iscariot of course. He reminded them of the things He'd explained before... that He'd be sending the Holy Spirit to come to take His place (Acts 1:4). He said they'd be *baptized*, like someone being baptized in water by John. Wow. They didn't fully understand but this sounded pretty extreme, all consuming, and a truly defining moment. He said they should wait in Jerusalem for this wonderful gift that God would give to them.

Then He referred to the huge, challenging but awesome responsibility that they now shared with Him... the Task of taking the whole Good News about Him to the immediate neighborhood, the larger community and out to the scattered ethnic groups around the world (Acts 1:8).

This was not something they could hope to do with their own limited wisdom and strength. They wouldn't care enough, be patient and disciplined enough, or have the insights needed to communicate His Narrative with others. But God's Spirit can and does. He has all of God's infinite love, patience, faithfulness, wisdom and power at His disposal. And He was going to make it available to them... and of course to *us* who have inherited the ongoing Task from the Apostles. Jesus said that when the Spirit came on to them He'd empower them for the Task they now had before them.

These were the final things Jesus said to them before disappearing up into a cloud as He returned to be with His Father in Heaven... where He is now. The rest of God's Narrative communicates what the Spirit taught them, and then guided them, and others, to do over the next few decades as they obediently took on that Task.

? DISCUSSION POINTS

1. In a friendly, open conversation, what would you say to someone who believes that the so-called sacraments (the bread and wine) become the actual flesh and blood of Jesus in a Catholic Mass?

2. What are some of the ways that you believe the Holy Spirit guides you? Are you conscious, in a daily way, of His role in your life?

3. Why do you think that the Task committed to the disciples by Jesus is not yet finished? If we were to ask Him about that as His Church, what do you think His response would be to us?

2.9 God's Narrative continued – Acts

 OBJECTIVES OF THIS TUTORIAL

The Narrative of God's Word continues in this tutorial, which is an introduction to the book of Acts.

A new part of the journey

We are about to launch into the next amazing part of God's Narrative - His true Account of who He is and of what He is about.

We have already covered the first part of that Narrative; not every detail, but touching on key events and characters, and tracing the important threads that led up to the coming of Jesus, the Saviour. We also took an overview of the remarkable accounts of Jesus' life and work that culminated in His crucifixion and resurrection. Now, as we've heard, He returned to His Father in Heaven… but the Narrative is by no means over. Everything *before* Jesus was leading up to Him and everything *afterward* can be said to flow out from Him. He is the central point of history, and nothing can be truly understood if it doesn't take Him into account.

We can be very grateful that God made sure we would have a record of what took place in the days, months and years after Jesus left the earth. It was written of course by Luke, one of Jesus' four official biographers, 'official' in the sense that they were appointed by God. Later on, in a reference by a colleague and traveling companion we find out that Luke was a doctor. The account he penned of what took place, as Jesus' followers reached out with the Good News, would become known as *Acts of the Apostles*, or simply *Acts*. A more accurate name might be "The *Acts* of the Holy Spirit through the Apostles". It's possible to see a reflection of Luke's medical training in the methodical way he draws together his own and other eyewitness accounts of events. It is an accurate record of events which would have - and still are having - an enormous historical significance for the world.

History that is also *our* story...for today

So Acts is historical, but if we *only* see it as history, even 'Church History' - at least if by that we mean dry facts and figures about events long past - then we miss out on the enormously important and relevant lessons that we can glean.

Or maybe it becomes just another 'Bible book' - a compilation of detached texts and devotional readings. It's easy to forget that this is a *true* story about *real* people in *actual* places, who faced challenges very similar to ours and who were given resources that we also have available to us. Or else it gets reduced to a list of references in sermons and lectures and youth group talks. Nothing wrong with proof texts, bulleted points and Power Point slides, just so long as we remember that Acts is the record of some of the most exciting and far-reaching things that have ever happened on this planet.

But these are not just fascinating things that happened a long time ago in a distant place to some other people. This is, in fact, *our* story, *our* history. It's where we can find out what makes us *us*. Not that we want to spend our time 'navel gazing', as the saying goes... introspectively obsessed with ourselves. But aligning our view of ourselves with who God says we are, moves us a long way towards actually being that, being those people, being and doing what He designed us for.

Part of our identity

There are many elements to the mosaic that forms our individual sense of identity - a lot of layers that add up to the picture we have of ourselves. These are put in place, often without us noticing, by our experiences of our families, our friends, our formative environment, the people we've mixed with in our lives, the larger culture and its media, and so on. But when we put our faith in Jesus Christ, we were *born again*...became, in the most fundamental ways, new people. So what is our identity in light of that? How does this new identity fit in with, or perhaps conflict with, the ways we've always seen ourselves and been seen by others?

Because this issue of identity is so very important, when we followed God's Narrative for *the first time*, we highlighted those parts that helped us understand who God is... then, in light of that, we looked at who we are in our natural state - as His fallen, corrupted race of image bearers. But then, in our *second brief overview*, we focused a lot of our attention on who God says we are *now*, as those who've been restored to a relationship with Him through the death and resurrection of His Son, Jesus Christ.

As we move ahead into *the Acts Narrative*, this new identity is clarified further as we observe the beginnings of a new entity that joins together all those who are His people under the New Covenant... His united people, or *Church*. So this is not cold, sterile theology but relevant and exciting realities that relate directly to how we see ourselves, how we view others who also believe, and how we relate to the rest of the human race.

The Holy Spirit's part

Something directly related to the inception of this new Entity is the arrival and ongoing role of the Holy Spirit. His presence will prove, in the course of the Narrative, to be so integrated into the lives of believers - individually and as a group - that it's not possible to think of them without including Him. They are *who they are* because He is *who He is*.

But it is not just *their story*… as we've already said, this is also *our* story, because He connects us with the rest of God's family - across space and also through time. His presence in the Acts Narrative links it directly and personally with our 21st century narratives.

Two paradigms in conflict

Another important transition was also taking place. But it's one that, on the face of it, we might wrongly assume is not all that relevant to our daily lives… something just of academic interest to theologians. As we know, the Old Covenant was made between God and a particular ethnic group who were the descendants of one man, Abraham. Now another Covenant had replaced it, this one initiated through Jesus' blood, through His death. And this one would not be defined by ethnicity or ancestry at all but by faith, and by the Holy Spirit.

Of course, as the Acts Narrative records, this created tensions between those still clinging on to the Old Covenant paradigm and those who were clearly seeing the implications of the New.

But why should we find these threads in the Narrative interesting and how does all this relate to us in very different places, centuries later?

Well for one thing, even though we might not face pressure to go to the Temple and sacrifice like the early Jewish Christians did, the underlying principles are still relevant. It's important for us to know, as New Covenant people, how we should view God's Law that He gave with the Old Covenant. How free are we under this new Agreement…or should we be trying to follow the Law? From the Acts account of the first believers' journey towards answering these questions we get important insights about how we should approach large chunks of the Old Testament Narrative… and also clues about how God wants *us* to live today.

The completion of the Narrative

During this inaugural and transitional period the Holy Spirit was also guiding some of Luke's co-workers to write what, along with *Acts* and *the Gospels*, would become God's revelation for the New Covenant...the compilation of books that in English we refer to as the *New Testament*.

A lot of it, as we know, is in the form of extensive, carefully written letters - *Epistles* is the older English term that has stuck - sent to individuals and groups of believers. Luke's history is important to us because it gives us important background details that help us understand the specific contexts, problems and questions the different authors had in mind as they wrote.

Even though *we* might reach for an electronic device instead of a papyrus scroll to access the truths written down by the Apostles... and even though our 21st century lives might look very different from what the first generation of believers faced, the Acts Narrative makes it clear that the challenges are basically the same. And so that's one reason we want to look at this now; it sets the stage for the rest of God's Narrative contained in the New Testament, and shows us that God's revelation is not abstract theory but real encouragement and guidance for His children no matter when or where they are on this earth.

The Gospel starts its journey

Another reason all this is compelling for us is because the changes under the New Covenant launched the Gospel's outward journey from its Jewish, Jerusalem source... out along the roads and shipping routes of the Roman Empire... through the medium of the Greek language that was so widespread... transported out by the Apostles of course, but also by Silk Road merchants, incense traders, sailors, Roman soldiers, slaves, itinerant workers and animal herders.

The Good News unleashed by a potent combination of Jesus' authority, the Spirit's empowerment, and His people's obedience broke down cultural and linguistic barriers wherever it went. It began to draw people who didn't look at all Jewish, who spoke strange languages and whose food was anything but kosher. This outward impetus of the Gospel that Luke records for us...its spread to the non-Jewish peoples - the Gentiles - in the areas dominated by the Roman Empire, would continue on and eventually bring it to us. But as significant as that is for each of us personally, there's a lot more to the picture than how we've benefited. The Task is not completed. What began then is still going on... the Holy Spirit is still challenging and equipping His people to complete the work the Apostles began.

One of the most prominent characters in Luke's story about the Apostles and the early Church was a man called Paul. After his dramatic conversion, this former enemy of anything or anyone promoting the New Covenant would go on to be its greatest advocate. Some of what Luke writes are his first hand accounts - a blog might be today's equivalent - of traveling around the Mediterranean area with Paul and others, looking for opportunities to tell people the Good News. God has provided a way back to Himself through His own Son who lived recently in Palestine, was crucified by the Romans, but who now lives again as the rightful ruler of the world.

When some from towns like Ephesus or Corinth or an area like Galatia came to faith in Jesus Christ, Paul and friends would gather them together and share the whole of God's Narrative with them. As they were equipped with Truth, these groups of people developed a sense of corporate identity... as distinct groups within the larger community. They grew stronger in the faith and could utilize the skills, abilities and insights given to them as a group by the Holy Spirit. They were also increasingly able to care for their own needs as a 'body' of believers, to worship their Lord, to feed themselves from His Word, and to be His witness in their immediate communities and beyond. And so a pattern was established... a model that would look different in *form* from place to place but would remain unchanged in its *essence* and *function*. So as we trace the Acts account of how Paul and the other Apostles went about fulfilling the Task Jesus had entrusted to them, we can glean invaluable insights into how we should be going about that same Task today. And by seeing their commitment, their passion and their willingness to sacrifice for the sake of their Master, we are inspired to do the same.

GOD'S NARRATIVE CONTINUED – ACTS

❓ DISCUSSION POINTS

1. Do you feel you have an understanding of how the Acts Narrative fits into the whole of God's Narrative? Have you spent time thinking about or been exposed to teaching that clarifies how the overall themes in God's Word flow from the Old Testament, through the Gospels, into Luke's *Acts* account and then on to the rest of the New Testament?

➡ ACTIVITIES

1. Ask and record the answers three different Christian friends give to these questions (try to ask people from a range of backgrounds) and then also include your personal responses:

a) How long is it since you have heard teaching that covers the book of Acts chapter-by-chapter and/or verse-by-verse?

b) On a scale of 1-10 how relevant do you feel the book of Acts is to your daily life?

c) Do you believe that God was doing anything particularly unique during the period covered in the Acts account, or are things still essentially the same in that respect today?

d) Do you believe that God is adding to His special Revelation today, or was that completed with what is in the New Testament?

e) In what ways do you feel your church closely follows, or is different from, the pattern in the New Testament?

2.10 The arrival of the Holy Spirit

 OBJECTIVES OF THIS TUTORIAL

The Narrative continues from Acts - this time we look at the account in God's Word of the coming of the Holy Spirit on the day of Pentecost.
The portions of Scripture referred to in this tutorial are: **Acts 1:5,9-26, 2:1-41, John 14:16-17**

Last time
We scanned the road ahead...to chart the journey we're embarking on as we follow Luke's account of the Acts of the Apostles. We considered just how important this record is for us as 21st century believers - that it isn't just dusty old history or facts for academic theology. In this account we continue to learn important elements of who we are as individual members of Jesus' *Body*, or *Church* here on the earth. We also anticipate with excitement the opportunity to learn - or be reminded of - important principles for us, the current generation of believers, and how we can play our part in the Task that Jesus entrusted to His disciples as He left the earth.

"Why are you standing there...?"
But for now, the disciples and a few others of Jesus' closest relatives and friends are hanging out together in a room in Jerusalem. The talk is all about what happened just hours before, and what it means for the future. Gradually more people come upstairs and join them in the room that has become something of a headquarters for Jesus' followers in Jerusalem. It's a good-sized space, but it's crowded now with everyone gathered there (Acts 1:12,13).

They're all people who over the last few years have come to firmly believe that Jesus is the Messiah and God's substitute Lamb - the ultimate and final sacrifice for their sins that God has accepted completely. After all, God raised Him back from death - how could you not believe in Him now? Most, if not all of them, had seen Him at different times in the last six weeks. They'd all speculated that surely now He'll lead a movement to throw out the Roman occupying forces and put Himself on the Throne of the nation. But obviously that wasn't the plan, at least not immediately…because He's gone!

His eleven disciples have told and retold the story of how they'd been over on the Mountain of Olives just today talking to Him face to face. "And then suddenly", they said, "we're just watching Him go up, and then looking at the spot in the clouds where He's disappeared. Who knows how long we stood there… we were all just feeling like, what now? What do we do next? Then we were startled to find there were two angels standing there right beside us. They looked like people, like men, but in really white clothes. We knew straight away they had to be from God. They even had a bit of a joke with us. They said, 'Hey you guys from Galilee, why are you standing there staring up at the sky?'

They said that Jesus had gone to Heaven, but that He'd return in the same way He went (Acts 1:9-11). So that at least is encouraging. We're not sure how long He'll be gone…a few months, or years? He said that only God the Father sets dates and times for stuff to happen. Anyway, we reminded ourselves that He'd told us to wait here in Jerusalem until He sends the One He promised… to give us power He said, to be His witnesses everywhere."

As new people come upstairs to the room the story is repeated for them. Luke's account says that they prayed…in fact, they kept praying. It was their default response to whatever happened. They would talk with God about it, voicing their worship and also asking Him for His involvement in everything (Acts 1:14). After a while Peter speaks up and says it's time for them to choose a replacement for Judas the betrayer, who by now has killed himself. Eventually a guy called Matthias, who traveled with them regularly as they followed Jesus, is appointed as the twelfth Apostle. Very clearly they have a sense of the importance of the role they have as Apostles - they are going to lead the group's efforts to represent the Master and to fulfill the Task He's entrusted to them (Acts 1:15-26).

The arrival of the Holy Spirit

It's a week and a half later, the day of Pentecost - the Jewish feast to celebrate and thank God for the barley harvest. The disciples and other believers in Jerusalem have gathered in the morning in the same room. Luke's record reflects the suddenness of what comes next. Everyone hears a loud noise. What's happening? It sounds like wind roaring down from overhead, filling the room. And what's that in the air? Flames… now they've settled above everyone's heads… but without burning them (Acts 2:1-4).

We're reminded of another time centuries before, when Moses was confronted with the alarming sight of a bush with flames dancing around it that didn't burn it up… God's presence there, he was told, made it holy ground. Then months later he was climbing the same mountain, having left the Israelites down below. This time the whole mountain was shaking and the air was full of lightning and the sound of thunder. God again was demonstrating His holiness as He initiated the First Covenant.

Now, at these early stages of the New Covenant, God's holy presence is once again represented in the physical world with fire. But instead of it being *external* and a cause for *fear*, the Holy Spirit's presence for Jesus' followers is *internal* and reason for real joy.

We're also reminded of God's glory, shining in the Most Holy Place in the Tabernacle. Then, God had graciously come to live among His people. Now, on this remarkable morning in Jerusalem, God's Spirit has come to live with His people under the New Covenant. But it won't be in a room in a tent, shut off from His chosen people because of their sin. This time He's actually come to live *in* these members of His image-bearing race who He has given so much for. And He can gladly do this because He has pronounced them to be holy and righteous through Jesus' death.

Luke's Account and the ongoing Narrative make it clear that the Holy Spirit has also come on this auspicious day to live in them not only as individuals, but also as a group. A very appropriate and helpful term for this group - one that the Narrative will frequently use - is *Body*. Another word used extensively by the writers is borrowed from Greek culture - *Ecclesia* - people called out from their homes or activities to gather for a specific purpose. Most English translators have chosen the word "Church", but centuries of western history has tended to weigh this term down with a lot of unfortunate baggage.

But the important point here - and one that helps us sort through all the potential confusion about the whole idea of 'church' - is that from the very beginning, God's people on earth were united and defined by their relationship with His Spirit. All those that were His then, and since, have had the permanent presence of God's Spirit in them individually and corporately. So that means *us*. We are, as the Narrative will declare elsewhere, God's Temple… in other words, the special, holy, place here on earth that is reserved just for Him.

When we put our faith in Jesus Christ, God claims us as His own… His Holy Spirit moves in to make our lives His home. He doesn't overpower our personalities, but He co-exists with our own spirits and gently works with us to teach, guide and encourage. And, in the process, He merges us as individuals with the larger Body of His people… He is the blood, if you like, that courses through the veins of His called-out group of people, giving life and unifying us for Christ's purposes.

So what Jesus said He'd do, had happened. Just before His death, when the disciples were disturbed and discouraged, He promised to send Someone who'd encourage them and guide them into Truth (John 14:16-17). And then again recently, just ten days ago, as He was leaving to return to Heaven, He'd reconfirmed that promise, saying they would be baptized with the Holy Spirit (Acts 1:5). This dramatic event at the inception of the Church left them in no doubt that the Spirit had come. The experience was all consuming…a genuine "baptism of fire". As a result, they all felt the Holy Spirit directing their words and actions completely… "filled" is the term Luke and other Narrative writers use.

We too can be filled - we can allow Him to guide us by His truth and respond to His gentle promptings, regardless of how we might *feel* at a given moment. But in this wonderful, wild, exciting time at the beginnings of the journey for the new Church and the Good News it was entrusted with, the Spirit's filling had some very special and dramatic results. Suddenly they could speak, and understand, languages they'd never known before. This is enormously significant and provides a signpost for how God was intending to continue with His great Rescue plan in this new era.

On this day of Pentecost - the day for celebrating a harvest - God was demonstrating in a most emphatic way that this New Covenant would not be just for the Jewish people, would not just be proclaimed in Hebrew or even Aramaic… but would go out to the ethnic non-Jews, the *goyim* in Hebrew or *Gentiles* that English would borrow from Latin. And, because He is the communicating, revealing God, His Narrative that culminates in the Good News about Jesus, would be communicated in languages that spoke to people's hearts. God has always graciously taken it on Himself, to speak to humans in their languages and in ways they can understand.

Now the Spirit is telling the members of the newly established *Ecclesia* - the Gathering, the Church - that they would go out communicating God's Good News Narrative to the nations in ways that would be clearly understandable to their audience. But they would not have to undertake this Task on their own… He would give them the resources to get it done. Now the formerly confused and frightened group is confident. They begin to tell everyone they can see in the narrow streets around. And, Luke records that there was an immediate harvest then and there. God-fearing Jews who've traveled to Jerusalem from all over the Mediterranean area for the Passover are still here for Pentecost (Acts 2:5-13).

They hear the noise of something going on that's reverberating off the stone walls and overhanging buildings: "What's going on?" - "I'm going to climb up here where I can see." - "It's that group from Galilee, the followers of Jesus." - "What language is that? They're babbling, must be drunk…and so early in the morning, pathetic" - "No, no, I can understand, that's the language of where my family settled, out in Mesopotamia." - "Yes, and that one over there is speaking our trade language in Cappadocia." - "Hey, now this one is speaking Egyptian."

And Peter, by now the established spokesman of the Jesus group, gets where he can be seen and loudly makes himself heard (Acts 2:14-41). "Come on, we're not drunk…at this time of the morning? What's happening here was foretold centuries ago. This is God's Spirit who has come to us like wine or oil being poured out. It all has to do with Jesus of Nazareth who the religious leaders collaborated with the Romans to execute recently. But He is the long-awaited Messiah. The One King David spoke of. He is the Lord! The fact is, it was *you* - His own people - who crucified Him. But God raised Him again and now He's gone back to the place of highest honor in Heaven. And now He's sent His Spirit. So that's what's going on here."

The message strikes home. They repent… recognize their sin, realize that they've been trying to make themselves righteous before God through their own efforts; they put their faith in Jesus the Messiah as God's substitute who took their sins on Himself. Some 3000 people are baptized and become a part of this *Body,* this *Church* that is not even really a day old. Those people are our brothers and sisters… we're joined to them despite the intervening centuries by the Holy Spirit who lived in them, just like He lives in us today.

THE ARRIVAL OF THE HOLY SPIRIT

? DISCUSSION POINTS

1. In your own words, explain what it means when we say that the Holy Spirit lives *in* people, lives *in* **you**. Do you think that who you are, the things that make you a distinct person, are lessened somehow by this?

2. Explain what you understand God's purpose was in bringing the *Ecclesia* - the Church - into being. (Note: don't go beyond what we've covered in the Narrative so far and try to tie your answer into the themes that have been highlighted.)

3. What is your personal response to the thought that as the great Communicator, God is graciously reaching out through His *Body* the Church, to share the Good News in whatever way is most understandable to people? Do you find anything in this that might help define a value or commitment for your own life? If so, how would you describe it?

→ ACTIVITIES

1. Write up to 500 words explaining your understanding of (a) *baptism* of the Spirit (b) being *filled* with the Spirit...are they the same thing, or different and if so how? (Note: If you are not quite sure what you believe about these issues, please state that. Also, you're obviously free to look up any resources you like, but please describe your own viewpoint rather than cutting and pasting someone else's opinion.)

2.11 The meaning of Baptism

 OBJECTIVES OF THIS TUTORIAL

At this point in the narrative of Acts, three thousand people are baptized. This tutorial discusses baptism, looking at Jewish baptism, John's baptism, and the true meaning of baptism under the New Covenant.
The portion of Scripture referred to in this tutorial is: **Matthew 3:11,13, Acts 2:37, Acts 2:41**

Last time
We found the disciples in an upstairs room in Jerusalem where they and other followers of Jesus regularly gathered in the days after His return to Heaven. On the morning of the Jewish festival day called Pentecost the Holy Spirit came in a special way to the world, to permanently live in the *Body* of believers, and in each one individually. This fulfilled Jesus' promise to the disciples that He'd send a Replacement for Himself. As a sign of His coming, the Spirit gave them the ability to speak in other languages, which were recognized by people from different countries staying in Jerusalem at the time. Three thousand people were saved and added to the new Church that day.

Why baptize the new converts?
The Narrative says that all of those 3000 people were baptized (Acts 2:41). So, picture the scene. For the Apostles and the rest of Jesus' small band of followers there in Jerusalem it has been an incredible day. Since Jesus left, the questions must have swirled around in all their minds and no doubt constantly came up in their conversations and prayers. What did the future hold for them as a group? Would they just end up being seen as an obscure sect of Judaism that faded quickly away? Now of course everything has changed with the Holy Spirit's arrival. Suddenly hundreds and hundreds of people who'd previously been hostile, or at least indifferent, were joining them! They too have put their faith in Jesus as the Christ, and have accepted His sacrifice on their behalf!

When have things ever changed for a group of people so quickly and dramatically? So then why, in the middle of this tumultuous excitement and new hope do they start baptizing people? Obviously for them it is pretty important, or they wouldn't be making the effort. What puts it so high on their priorities, and what do the new believers understand it is all about? If it was so important to the Apostles on this inaugural day of His *Body* to which we also belong, then surely it must be important for us today to understand why.

Jewish baptism

It is helpful for us to consider the background context and the things the disciples were processing. Baptism or ritual immersion, known as *mikveh*, has long been a part of Jewish religious custom. The *Torah* - the Law God gave Moses spelling out the conditions for the Old Covenant - demanded a complete washing of the body for a number of things… for example, people who'd become ceremonially unclean somehow, or before a priest could carry out certain tasks. The *Talmud* - the Jewish civil and ceremonial traditional law - also requires the *mikveh* immersion for other instances such as a bride before her wedding, or a woman after childbirth. Before bringing a sacrifice, a man goes through the ritual full body cleansing. Also, a Gentile man wanting to become a Jew is required by the priests to go through ritual immersion as well as circumcision. There are a number of designated pools, or *mikvot* as they are known, sunk into the rock around the Temple area - evidence of which can still be seen today, 2000 years later (picture at right).

John's baptism

They also have another kind of baptism still quite fresh in their minds. All the disciples are familiar with the message that John, Jesus' cousin, was preaching a few years ago. Most had been drawn along with the crowds who'd gone to the uninhabited stretch of the Jordan river where John was preaching and challenging people to prepare their hearts for the coming of the Messiah.

We can assume that along with others, prepared to publicly acknowledge their guilt before God, they had each gone down into the river, then under the water, to represent their need for complete spiritual cleansing by the Promised One from God. We don't know, because the Narrative doesn't tell us, whether John said any specific words or even exactly what role he played in these baptisms. It may have been that individuals immersed themselves, as was traditional in the *mikveh* ritual cleansing. Certainly he was seen to have authority in the process as the teacher of God's Truth because the text records him saying "I baptize with water…" and also that "Jesus went from Galilee to the Jordan River *to be baptized by John.*" (Matthew 3:11,13)

The Spirit's guidance was available

So the Apostles were aware of the ritual immersions related to the Old Covenant, and to the baptism associated with John's preaching...but those were different. One was for a system that they knew had now been superseded by the New Covenant Jesus had initiated through His blood...as He'd so memorably represented with a cup of wine in their meal together just before His arrest. The other was to prepare people and demonstrate repentance in the time leading up to Jesus publicly declaring Himself as the Promised Messiah. So it's not as though there are no cultural, historic and even 'Narrative' threads tying this new Dawn of the Church with the past, but everything needs to be reinterpreted now in light of how God's purposes are to play out under the New Covenant.

God remains unchanged, of course, but His Son's coming to the earth and then all He achieved here has brought about a landmark shift in...well, in *everything*. The Apostles are no doubt just beginning to glimpse the scope of the changes and to understand some of the implications. Jesus has left them to lead His Group as decisions are made about how things should be done. But this is new territory. How are things to be done now? Should they just follow the old *forms*, the Jewish traditions? Should they invent new ones? What, for example, should they do when someone says they have repented and put their faith in Jesus as the Christ? If only He were still here to show the way.

Oh, but what a comfort to remember that God's Spirit is with them permanently now. They don't have to work things out for themselves. Jesus had said the Spirit would lead them into all Truth. So they can rely on Him to help them know how to function...to know how to think about things in this new era. He can guide them as they guide the *Ecclesia* - God's called out people. And they'd already experienced how this was supposed to work. First up, He'd given Peter exactly the right words for addressing the crowds that morning...the things that would convince them of their sin and need for salvation through God's Son, Jesus. And then, when the people - *pierced to the heart* as Luke would later describe it (Acts 2:37) - were calling out asking them what they should do, the Spirit had reminded him of what Jesus said just before He went back to heaven. He said that based on the authority God had given Him, He was sending *them* out - His disciples - to make disciples of people from all the world's ethnic groups - some of which were represented there in the crowd - and that they were to baptize them in the name of the Father, Son and Holy Spirit (Matthew 28:18-19).

What baptism means under the New Covenant

So that's what they did to some 3000 people, and as each one was baptized they were making a public statement that through their faith they were now permanently associated with Jesus of Nazareth and His group of followers. It seems likely that the Apostles also explained to the believers and any other observers what would later be explained in written form in God's Word. This act of baptism doesn't itself *do* anything. It doesn't save anyone or change their status in God's eyes. But as a physical action it provides us with a powerful illustration of something amazing that we know has already happened:

"This pool, the water you see here, represents Jesus' death and the grave. When Jesus hung on that cruel cross just a few months ago, He was representing this person before God. So now as they go down under the water it is a picture of His death and burial that they've participated in through faith. They have died with Him and their sins have been dealt with. Now, watch as they come up out of the water. It represents what has happened… God has included them in Jesus' resurrection. It's just like when He came out of the tomb. God raised Him again and rolled away the stone because the payment for sin was completed. Sin and death couldn't hold Him. And so it is for this person. Now they have been raised to a new life with our dear Master. And they can enjoy a relationship with God because of Him. They have God's Holy Spirit living in them as do all of us who are His people." This baptism that the disciples initiated then at the dawn of the Church, carries on today for all of those who, as Jesus' disciples, become part of that Church.

? DISCUSSION POINTS

1. Does the description of baptism here line up with what you have been taught previously?

2. Do you feel this view of baptism is consistent with the flow of God's Narrative, as it has described His character and purposes so far?

3. If you have been baptized, what was your understanding at the time? Was it done in such a way as to reflect the rich illustration of a believer dying, being buried and then being resurrected with Jesus?

4. Do you feel that it is important to be baptized as a believer through immersion, or do you see this as one of the "negotiables" of our faith?

5. Do you have any thoughts on *who* should baptize someone else? Is there anything in the Narrative so far that might guide us in this?

2.12 Life in the New Church at Jerusalem

 OBJECTIVES OF THIS TUTORIAL

This tutorial looks in detail at the description of the Early Church from Acts. The portion of Scripture referred to in this tutorial is: Acts 2:42-47

Last time

We considered the significance of the Apostles baptizing the 3000 new believers in Jerusalem on the day of Pentecost. We asked ourselves why this was significant and reflected on what kind of baptism was appropriate for the New Covenant. As with other areas, the fledgling Church would need the Holy Spirit's help to reinterpret baptism's significance and meaning in this new era. Although it might bear an outward resemblance to what happened under the Old Covenant and during John's ministry, it would have an entirely new meaning under the New. Baptism, then and now, represents a believer's identification with Jesus' death, burial and resurrection to a new life.

Invaluable principles embedded in the Acts account

Luke continues his Acts account with a brief description of what life looked like for that first group of believers in Jerusalem. Any details that we find in these accounts of the early *Ecclesia* or Church are very important and well worth our attention. It's not that we are looking to exactly replicate the way they did everything… the physical and cultural landscape was obviously quite different from ours.

From the beginning God has been writing and telling the true Narrative of who He is in real places, events and particularly the people of the world He created. He does not lock us arbitrarily into the outward *forms* of a particular historical or cultural setting. Instead, the Holy Spirit guides His people from different places and times in how to live out His Narrative in their own lives as they worship Him and try to be effective witnesses for Him. This is part of the genuine collaboration He invites His people into and then equips them for, as they're willing.

So when we scrutinize the Acts Narrative it is for the purpose of seeing how the Apostles guided the early Church as they tried to be all that they knew their Lord wanted them to be. As we observe the way they did things, what we're keen to identify is the underlying principles that the Holy Spirit was teaching them. We know that these principles will line up with the threads of the Narrative that we have been tracing all the way through - who God is, why He created man, how He deals with anything that violates His perfect holy standards, what His intentions are, the kind of relationship He wants with us, and so on. But now, we want to understand how the Holy Spirit was helping the Apostles to guide that first generation of Christ's *Body* in applying that truth under the New Covenant in their time and place.

Those are obviously important insights for us because we are called on to live out that same truth in *our* time and place. Also, if we are to be well equipped to contribute to His Task that has passed down to us from the Apostles, we need to know how to guide others as they are joined to His *Body* and also become contributors to His purposes.

They were eager to hear the Apostles' teaching

The New Living Translation, which is what we're using for the text of the Narrative, translates into English the next part of Luke's account like this; "All the believers devoted themselves to the apostles' teaching, and to fellowship, and to sharing in meals (including the Lord's Supper), and to prayer." (Acts 2:42).

The first thing highlighted here is that the believers highly value coming together and listening to the group of men Jesus had specially authorized to speak for Him. Remembering of course that the written Narrative, God's Word for the New Covenant - or *Testament* - is not yet available at this point. So, just as Jesus had said would happen, the Spirit is constantly reminding the Apostles of things that Jesus taught and did during His time with them. Then in the regular times they are together with the other believers, they are passing on what they've remembered. But they're not just reminiscing - although no doubt everyone who'd spent time with the Lord has very fond memories to share.

When the Church is gathered, the Apostles are reviewing what Jesus taught them… but now they understand so much more and are able to explain it to the group. At the time, when they were with Him, they knew He was telling them really important things, knew it was true, believed Him completely…but often felt like they were groping in the dark to understand. Now they feel the Spirit making those things clear, like opening the blinds one by one in a dark room.

And He's also giving them new insights. As they read the Old Testament Narrative these days, they're seeing everywhere threads God embedded there that point forward to

Jesus the Christ. Every day, it seems, they are blown away to stumble upon something there, which they can now see was fulfilled in the life, death and resurrection of Jesus.

But when the Apostles gather the believers, they are not just sharing theoretical, abstract truths, they're also helping everyone apply those things... to think through how they should live now, right here in Jerusalem - how to act and speak, how to relate to others. They're helping them grapple with the freedom and the responsibilities of living under the New Covenant - something that's going to take time and revelation from God's Spirit to understand. Everyone is excited by this process of hearing Truth revealed. They feel as though they are on a journey together, with the Apostles out in front and God's Spirit leading them all.

The great news for us is that the things the Spirit was teaching the Apostles were written down over the next decades as part of God's Narrative - the *New Testament*. He has made sure that all the important truths He helped them uncover and pass on to the 1st century believers are also available to us in the 21st century. What's more, the Holy Spirit is eager to help us understand and apply truth to our lives, today. And - as we'll see - He gives the ability and authority to men within local bodies of believers to ensure that everyone understands the Apostles' teaching and can relate it to real-life situations.

They enjoyed a special relationship

In his brief description of what was happening with that first group of believers in Jerusalem, Luke also talks about the way they were relating to each other (Acts 2:42-47). Jesus had told the disciples that it would be their care and affection for each other that would show the world they were His people. And now, bound together by the Holy Spirit, it was proving to be that way. Luke used a word - often translated as "fellowship" in English - *koinonia*, that conveys the idea of closeness and particularly of sharing something in common. In other words, they enjoy relating to each other because of what they have in common... which, the more they think about it, is a great deal.

They have Jesus as their Saviour and Master in common; they all have the Holy Spirit binding them together; they are developing a very strong sense of a shared identity; they all feel they're on a journey of learning Truth through the Apostles together; and they are all called to contribute to the Task of being Jesus' witnesses here in Jerusalem and further afield. So even though they're glad to be out talking with people about Jesus the Messiah around the Temple or in the market areas or where people congregate such as the different gates of Jerusalem, they also realize that it's important for them to have separate times together as an *Ecclesia*... as the Gathering of believers.

They ate together, remembering Jesus' sacrifice

Luke also mentions that when they got together they'd share food. Actually, the words in Greek he uses are literally "breaking bread". That was his shorthand way of referring to what would later be called "the Lord's Supper", or in some traditions even later, as "Communion". But from what we'll see later in the Narrative, it seems probable that the early Church remembered Jesus' sacrifice in that way when they were already eating a meal together. After all, as we'll remember, Jesus and His disciples were eating a meal - albeit the special one to mark the Passover - when He used bread to represent His body and a cup of wine for His blood that would initiate the New Covenant.

How often this should be done, the exact procedures to follow, and even what specific kinds of food and drink should be used to remind us of Jesus' sacrifice and victory at Calvary…these are issues that have been debated endlessly down through history. But the picture here is, in many ways, a simple one that we can learn from - those early believers regularly gathered and, conscious of all they had in common, they remembered their Lord's death together in the way He'd told them to. It's sad and unfortunate when people add their own ideas onto God's Narrative and create dogma about what has to be done in order to please Him. When in fact Jesus has already done everything to please His Father… our appropriate response is simply to trust in Him, remember Him, and be grateful, just like those first believers were.

They spent time praying together

Another real feature of the early *Ecclesia* Luke notes was how devoted they were to prayer. The Apostles and other followers of Jesus could not have missed how prayer was important to Him. Not as some formula, or empty ritual, but real, heartfelt communication with His Father. They had the record too from the Old Covenant with numerous instances of God's people speaking to Him.

After all, it's a very important part of fulfilling what we were created for. God made people in His image specifically so He can communicate with them and so they can respond. He delights in hearing His children acknowledging His creative power, His holiness, and His grace and mercy in their lives. Prayer is how we show our dependence on Him and how we communicate that we want His involvement in our lives. It is also a unifying thing for a group of believers - like that first one in Jerusalem - to hear each other presenting their combined worship and requests to God.

Further proof that this is an extraordinary time

Luke also says that the Apostles were performing "many miraculous signs and wonders" (Acts 2:43-47). God is demonstrating in this way that something extraordinary is taking place at this time. Just as He confirmed that Jesus was His Son through the extra-natural things He gave Him power to do, now He's showing that the authority to be Jesus' witnesses has been passed on to His followers. All of this has an enormous impact on the lives of the believers. They have a deep sense of awe and joy in their hearts. They're amazed at what they are part of. It completely reshapes their values. Those with land and houses or anything valuable are selling them and putting the money into a common fund, which is used to help anyone in need.

Their generosity and unity doesn't go unnoticed in the community. The general public, even if they don't put their faith in Jesus and join His followers, can't help but be impressed by them. And some *are* drawn to hear the Truth… each day more and more recognize their need of salvation, put their faith in Jesus, and are added to the *Ecclesia*.

LIFE IN THE NEW CHURCH AT JERUSALEM

? DISCUSSION POINTS

1. Explain in your own words what you believe we are supposed to get out of descriptions of the early Church. Are we meant to try to follow exactly the way they did everything? What factors should we be aware of as we try to sort out what we can appropriately apply today?

2. Obviously the Apostles had the primary authority in the Church as described in Acts. Reflect on the issue of authority, particularly in teaching, in the Church today. In your experience, do you see authority in teaching believers today bearing any resemblance to the picture we see in Acts? Identify any current issues (in Christianity and in the larger community) that you feel are a potential challenge for this authority.

➡ ACTIVITIES

1. Do some research on one of the following movements and in less than half a page reflect on any (1) *consistencies*, or (2) *contrasts* you see with the picture of the early Church in Acts:

Church Growth Movement

Seeker Friendly Church model

Emerging Church

Church Planting Movement (missions)

2.13 God demonstrates His power through the Apostles

> **OBJECTIVES OF THIS TUTORIAL**
>
> This tutorial looks in detail at several incidents from the book of Acts, where God spoke and worked through His Apostles to make His message clear.
> The portions of Scripture referred to in this tutorial are: **Acts chapters 3 and 4, Psalm 118:22**

Last time

We thought about how to glean principles from the book of Acts so that we can apply truth appropriately today. Luke gave a description of what was happening in the very early days for the Church in Jerusalem. The believers were keen to gather together and hear from the Apostles what the Holy Spirit had revealed to them. They enjoyed each other's company because of all they had in common. They often ate together and "broke bread", as Luke put it, to remember their Lord. And they put a real priority on prayer, spending time speaking to God.

A crippled man is healed through Peter and John

Now Luke describes an event that helps us understand how the Spirit was guiding the Apostles in their interactions with the wider community in Jerusalem (Acts 3:1-11). One afternoon, Peter and John are on their way to the Temple to take part in the three o'clock prayer service there. We know that these two guys are fishermen by trade, who responded to Jesus' invitation to follow Him, back in Galilee. By now they are some of Jesus' designated Apostles and key leaders in the early Jerusalem *Ecclesia*.

Both had the privilege later of contributing as authors to God's written Narrative in the form of letters they wrote to believers and churches… also in John's *Revelation* that records the amazing things God showed to him in visions while exiled on the Island of Patmos in the Aegean Sea.

The fact that they are on their way to the Temple is instructive for us. Peter and John, and the other Apostles, know full well that a New Covenant has replaced the Old. They are no longer sacrificing at the Temple, but neither are they rejecting, just for the sake of it, the practices of Judaism that don't contradict the Gospel. As time goes by, the Holy Spirit *will* open their eyes to some attitudes and practices they've wrongly brought over into the New paradigm - either through ignorance or fear of people… but that's in the future. For now, they continue to go to the Temple and join in the prayers which are, after all, offered to the true living God, who the believers know is the Father of the Lord Jesus.

This day Luke says that they are about to enter the Temple area by an entrance called *The Beautiful Gate*…well known by that name to his 1st century readers but not so easily identifiable today. It's safe to assume it is a well-used entrance because it's the spot where a crippled man chose to beg each day. This afternoon he's scrutinizing people, as beggars do, looking for someone to target. His eyes instinctively pick two men out from the crowd that is flowing past. They look like provincials, probably Galileans… weathered faces, and rough hands… no doubt fishermen. Perhaps he's seen them before…saw them before with Jesus of Nazareth. Maybe they'll feel generous, here in the big city to visit the Temple.

He gives his usual pitch, asking them for money. Oh, great, they're stopping, looking down. But no, it's a false alarm. They're saying they don't have any coins, but they'll give something else.

No thanks, don't need any clothes, or food… his eyes are already looking for the next target.

Now one of the fishermen is saying something about the name of Jesus of Nazareth, the One who created such a stir a few months back… the One the Romans crucified just outside the city wall. He'd thought a lot about that One. The guy called Jesus *the Christ*, the Messiah. Yes, that rings true. He felt sure He'd come from God. From all he'd heard, *that* One could heal him.

Now the man's telling him to get up and walk. Oh sure, I'd love to… what do you think I sit here for every day? But wait, what's going on? The fisherman has grabbed his hand, pulled him to his feet. For the first time in his life his legs are holding his weight! As he realizes what has happened he's flooded with a sense of elation and gratitude. He finds himself running, and jumping up and down, following the two men through the gate, yelling out to everyone about what's happened, praising God.

A crowd quickly gathers around them in the long porch on the eastern side of the Temple, the one called Solomon's Colonnade: "Hey, that's the guy who's always lying outside the gate begging." "No, that guy's a cripple, he can't walk." "I tell you, it's the same guy… says he's been healed." "It was those Galileans he's holding on to that did it."

You know, from the group who claim Jesus of Nazareth is the Messiah. This is incredible… maybe God is showing something."

Peter lays it on the line with a crowd at the Temple

Peter isn't going to let the opportunity slip. He starts speaking to the crowd that's growing by the second… and he doesn't hold back (Acts 3:12-26). First, he calls them "Israelites"… reminding them of their heritage as God's chosen people, the ethnic group who entered into a Covenant with God, who'd been entrusted with His Narrative, who'd been chosen as the line for the Promised Deliverer to come through.

He and John didn't make the man walk, he says… it was God, the same One Abraham, Isaac and Jacob knew… it was to bring glory to His servant, Jesus. Then Peter refers to something many standing there were involved in. After Jesus' arrest Pilate examined Him, and realizing He was an innocent man, proposed releasing Him. When the despised Gentile occupier was prepared to let Jesus go, it was they, the Jews, who'd demanded His death. They, who prided themselves on following the Law, had rejected the "Holy Righteous One" in favor of a known murderer.

Peter's words are sledgehammer blows raining down… he charges them with the truth: they killed the Author of life! But you know what? God raised Him back from death. It's the truth. We saw it… saw Him alive again. And as a matter of fact, it was because this man believed in His name that he was healed. And Peter challenges them to repent, to turn to God.

It must have struck them as strange to be told to repent and turn to God when they've been thinking of themselves as good, religious people, here at the Temple for afternoon prayers.

But being religious isn't enough; even being a good Jew won't cut it. The advantage they do have as Israelites is that by sending Jesus to them, God has given them the first chance to recognize their sin and put their faith in the way God has provided for forgiveness.

Time and space here don't allow us to glean everything we can from the words Peter spoke under the Holy Spirit's guidance. But as God's witnesses, we would be rewarded by reflecting on how he shapes his message so it *resonates* with his audience, *challenges* their existing worldview, gives the Spirit opportunity to *convict* them of their sin and lead them to *repentance*, and for them to face the stark *choice* the Gospel presents.

The Apostles are arrested, threatened, released

The commotion in the Temple area doesn't go unnoticed. Word quickly gets to the religious leaders that some followers of Jesus are making claims about Him having come back from death (Acts 4:1-22). Won't that troublemaker from Nazareth ever go away? Didn't they see to it that He was put to death?

That should have been the end of it… with His disciples just fading away. That's what happened with adherents of other populist leaders. But Jesus' followers suddenly seem bolder than ever.

Right! Time to teach these upstarts a lesson. They arrest Peter and John and confine them, probably within the Temple complex, in a chamber where guards can keep them under observation for the night. But although they've incarcerated the two apostles, they can't hold back the truth. In fact, this is a theme that flows through Luke's entire account. The Good News about Jesus continues to move out regardless of the obstacles put in its way.

God's Spirit has already used the words He helped Peter speak to the crowd. Luke records that many who heard his very direct challenge that afternoon put their faith in Jesus as the Messiah.

They realize they rejected the very One who fulfilled God's promises to their ancestors, the One the prophets had pointed towards, the Lamb of God who was the perfect sacrifice for their sins. Luke mentions that by now the believers number about 5000, enough to make the religious authorities nervous.

The next morning the entire Jewish Council meets. All the 'big guns' are present. The situation is obviously being taken very seriously. The two Galilean fishermen are brought in front of the formidable group of leaders, most of whom are highly educated, wealthy and self-assured.

They demand answers, their tone is menacing. "Whose authority do you think you're functioning under?" But the Apostles are not intimidated. God's Spirit is doing what He does… as an Insider, offering His help, encouragement, guidance and friendship…to God's people, as they go about God's purposes.

Peter, respectful but confident, tells the Supreme Jewish council that he and John are functioning under the authority of Jesus from Nazareth… the One they - those very leaders - had crucified, but who was also brought back to life by God. "If you want to know about how we helped the crippled man yesterday, if that's what you're asking about… well, it was in Jesus' name." And Peter quotes from a Jewish song that the leaders would have been very familiar with. He asserts with complete confidence that this song or *psalm* that is part of their Old Covenant Scriptures (Psalm 118:22) refers directly to Jesus when it says, "The stone that you builders rejected has now become the cornerstone." The message is clear. Because of their proud insistence on constructing something according to their own plans, these Jewish leaders had violently rejected the One God had chosen as the perfect, ultimate stone for His building. So whether it's about healing a crippled man or people being saved from their sin, God gives the authority through only One name in the entire universe - Jesus.

It's obvious that these two fisherman have not had specialized training in the Scriptures or in Jewish religious traditions. So that makes it even more amazing to the leaders that they can speak with such confidence. In a line of text loaded with significance, Luke says that the leaders recognized that these guys had spent time with Jesus. Even they, full of their own importance, achievements and position, have to acknowledge that people who followed Jesus would, of course, know a lot about the Scriptures.

Really, the Council find themselves at a loss. The guy who'd never walked before in over 40 years is standing there in front of them on his own two legs. It's the talk of Jerusalem. It was the same dilemma they faced with Jesus a few months ago…if they punish His disciples now it will probably start a riot. All they can do is rather weakly order them to never, ever, under absolutely no circumstances, use Jesus' name as their authority again!

Peter and John's response is polite, but you almost hear the incredulous amusement in their voices, "Would God want us to obey you or Him? Do you really think we're going to stop telling everyone about things we've actually seen and heard?" The Master's command is still ringing in their ears. He said they were to tell people about Him so they'd become His disciples… first in Jerusalem and then moving out from there. They are hardly likely to listen to any voices over His. After another hollow threat, the Council has no choice but to let them go.

Peter and John immediately report all this back to the rest of the believers. Before long, they are speaking to God together, acknowledging His amazing part in all these events (Acts 4:23-37). They also ask Him for courage not to be deterred by the threats of people. They want to keep sharing the Good News with others… and for Him to demonstrate His power through them so that people will have their needs met and come to know His Son, Jesus the Christ.

All of what has happened, including the threats from the authorities, only serves to unite the believers. They no longer see what they each have as their own exclusive possessions… it's been given to them to be shared. Their witness is increasingly powerful and effective. God shows that they are lined up with His purposes by blessing everything they're involved in.

❓ DISCUSSION POINTS

1. Without going beyond what we've covered in the Narrative so far, explain your understanding of why God gave the Apostles the power to perform miracles. Describe this in "Narrative terms" - in other words, in light of what has happened previously and what we can see that God is doing at this particular time in history.

2. How do you think you would have responded to the Jewish Supreme Council's commands and threats about speaking in Jesus' name? Do you tend to be fearful when you have an opportunity to share about Jesus or would you say that you tend to be bold? Are there times when we should speak out and others when we shouldn't? Please explain your answer.

➡ ACTIVITIES

Carefully read what Peter said to the crowd in the Temple. In a few sentences for each point, describe in your own words how he:

- Contextualized his message (i.e. described things in terms that would resonate with them)
- Built on Narrative foundations (i.e. what they already knew of God's Story)
- Challenged their worldview (i.e. assumptions that underpinned their beliefs, values and actions).

2.14 God guides the Church as they face challenges & persecution

 OBJECTIVES OF THIS TUTORIAL

This tutorial looks at the work of Apostles, elders, and deacons, and Stephen's sermon and death. We see how God guides His Church and its leaders as they face persecution from outside, sin from within, and as they learn to delegate roles and responsibilities according to His plan.
The portions of Scripture referred to in this tutorial are: **Acts chapters 5, 6 and 7**

Last time
We followed the account of God healing a crippled man through Peter and John. When a crowd gathered there in the Temple area to see what had happened, Peter challenged them strongly to recognize that Jesus, who they'd crucified, was the Messiah. The two former fishermen were arrested by the Supreme Council and the next morning they were warned not to speak in Jesus' name again. Peter and John replied that they would have to obey God and keep telling people about what they'd been eyewitnesses to. More people in Jerusalem believed in Jesus through these events and were added to the Church, which continued to strengthen and thrive.

Sin from inside and persecution from outside
In the Acts account, Luke next records two incidents that provide more insights into what God was doing at this point in history…how He was relating to the newly formed group that is Christ's *Body* or *Ecclesia* on earth (Acts Chapter 5). In the first, Luke describes how God deals decisively with a couple, attached to the Jerusalem church, who act deceptively and try to make themselves appear more generous than they actually are.

Although the results of sin among those claiming to be God's people today is rarely so dramatic and obvious as it was for the fledgling Church, the account tells us a lot about the view God takes of anything that dishonors His name or corrupts His Son's Body on earth.

The second incident again sees Peter and, this time, more of the Apostles, imprisoned overnight by the Jewish authorities. The next morning, despite the apparently intact jail security, the officials are shocked to hear that the leaders of Jesus' followers are out in the Temple area preaching. After being threatened and flogged, the Apostles are released - delighted, Luke records, to have had the privilege of suffering for the sake of their Master. None of these events discourage them from obeying Jesus' command to bring new followers - disciples - to Him. The text says that every day the Apostles were teaching whoever would listen, in open public forums and in individual homes. Without reaching for definite conclusions, it's worth noting in passing here that there's no mention of them trying to attract seekers to the meetings of the *Ecclesia* - from what we're told, the evangelism and teaching of anyone who's interested takes place outside the church gatherings.

Potential divisions emerge in the Church

What Luke records next is also highly instructive and relevant to us as members of Jesus' Body today...particularly as we try to obey His command to be witnesses and disciple-makers for Him in our local communities and out to the nations of the earth (Acts 6:1). Interestingly, we see that the group of early believers in Jerusalem is not as culturally or even linguistically homogenous as we might suppose. Certainly they share a history of Jewish ethnicity and religion, but there are significant differences among them. On the whole, the Hebrew or Aramaic speaking majority is from a conservative Jewish background. The Greek speakers are generally more liberal, having been influenced by *Hellenisation:* the Greek and, more recently, Roman cultural dominance in the Mediterranean 'world'.

These differences now represent potential fault lines along which the first divisions can occur in the so far unified *Ecclesia*... something that, sadly, has happened countless times since, for one reason or another, down through history. The text says there are "rumblings of discontent" in the Church. On the surface, the issue does not seem all that significant - the Greeks claim that their widows are not being cared for as well as the Hebrew women. But even relatively minor disputes can grow into serious problems if they're not handled right.

What will happen? Jesus had said that one of the distinctives of His people would be their love for one another. The Body, by definition, is meant to be *unified*. This is one of the reasons the Holy Spirit came - to join His New Covenant people together as *one*.

A new practical leadership role is instituted

So how will the Spirit respond to this issue? God's interaction with His people has always involved Him describing how things work within the reality He has created: the Author explaining the Narrative. His truth does not remain isolated in some mystical, spiritual realm… it works itself out in real life, it solves problems and provides practical frameworks within which we can fulfill His intentions. And, consistent with the pattern we've seen in God's dealings with humans from the beginning, He looks for opportunities to delegate real responsibility. This is entirely His choice as Creator… His *Sovereign* right. He graciously works with His faithful followers in genuine collaboration, rather than pushing them aside to deal with things Himself. This gets right down into the fundamental reasons for Him creating an image-bearing race in the first place.

Now these characteristics of God are playing themselves out in this new Chapter of His Narrative - the Group of Jesus Christ's blood bought people. Luke describes how the Apostles, led by the Spirit, act decisively with a practical solution that serves God's purposes for the Church (Acts 6:2-7). The Apostles have been gifted by the Spirit and placed within the Ecclesia specifically to serve it in certain ways. Their primary role is to feed the Body with spiritual sustenance… to share the Truth, God's Narrative, with authority and clarity so that it leads God's children into genuine worship, produces change in their values and behavior as needed, and equips them to contribute to His purposes. As leaders, they don't feel they have to micro-manage every aspect of the church's life. They are glad to follow God's pattern and what Jesus modeled for them by delegating responsibility to others.

They decide that seven men should be chosen to take leadership in the practical areas of the Church's function like the distribution of food. This will keep the Apostles free to focus on seeking God's guidance for themselves and for those in their care. But consistent with what they've seen from the Father and Son, these responsibilities will not just be handed out to anyone, nor will they be given on the basis of favoritism or social obligation. Whoever takes on these roles should clearly be submitting their lives to the Spirit's guidance and demonstrating wisdom in their dealings with others.

The Apostles don't act unilaterally or dictatorially, but instead put their plan before the group. The idea is supported and, significantly, it is the church body that chooses men among them who they feel are suitable… no doubt those who were already demonstrating an enthusiasm to serve, along with organizational skills. The names of the seven men chosen (Acts 6:5) suggests they were *Hellenists* - those with Greek cultural and language backgrounds - but this isn't certain because Palestinian Jews often had Greek names as well. In front of the group these men are recognized by the Apostles as those who'll take the lead in areas of *service* - a concept linked back to the practical roles of priests under the Old Covenant as they *served* God's people. In Greek, the term used is *diakonia* - "service" and *diakonos* "servant" - which of course has come into English as *deacon*. And so a pattern was established with God's guidance at the outset…two distinct but related ways to lead and serve the Church; as *Elders* - which the Apostles filled for the Jerusalem church - or as *Deacons*.

Stephen shows the pattern of the Jews' disbelief

What is described next in the Acts account (Acts 6:8-7:60) will have incredibly far-reaching results for the young Church, and for how it takes the next steps given to it by the Master. The Narrative focuses on one of the newly appointed servant leaders or *deacons* in the Jerusalem church.

Stephen is someone who is obviously experiencing God's grace himself and is able to help others see it as well. Along with it, the Spirit has given him a prominent role in demonstrating God's involvement in this new movement in Jerusalem…performing, as the text says, "amazing miracles and signs among the people". Trouble occurs when some antagonistic Hellenistic Jews realize they've come off second best in a theological debate with Stephen…what they don't know, of course, is that he has the advantage of the wisdom that comes from his constant companion, God's Spirit (Acts 6:8-14).

In a move very reminiscent of what happened to Jesus, these Jews persuade some others to accuse Stephen of blasphemy. The charges sound strikingly similar to what his Master was wrongly accused of. Selective fragments of the message are repeated, out of context of God's One Narrative…twisted and misapplied, they are made to sound heretical. The enemies of Jesus and His followers finally have what they've been waiting for…grounds on which to attack the movement that threatens their hold on the people. Stephen is arrested and brought before the Sanhedrin - the Supreme Council. The false charges are laid. How does he plead? Will he admit or deny the accusations?

With his face glowing, Stephen launches into a summary of the history of Abraham's descendants and their relationship with God (Acts 6:15-7:50). The conclusions he draws from this synopsis of the Old Covenant Narrative are anything but diplomatic. He clearly has no intention of ingratiating himself or avoiding any harsh treatment (Acts 7:51-53). They are stubborn he says, deaf and disobedient to the truth…resisting the efforts of God's Spirit to enlighten them, just like their ancestors so often did. They are no more God's people than the heathen Gentile people groups. They've persecuted and killed God's prophets, even killing the Messiah Himself.

Stephen is killed by the Jews

The Jewish leaders' supporters are beside themselves with rage… they hiss and jeer. But Stephen is no longer concerned with them. He's absorbed by something infinitely more compelling and wonderful (Acts 7:54-60). God's Spirit is allowing him to see beyond the boundaries of this limited world of the senses… to where God exists in all His glory. And look, there's His beloved Master, Jesus, standing next to His Father… in a place where He's fully honored and acclaimed.

Why can't the crowd see what is so real to him? Surely they see the Father and the Son there! But no, there's no one so blind as those who won't see, or as deaf as those who refuse to hear.

They cover their ears and shout to drown out what they're convinced is blasphemy. They want to make him stop…to revenge his accusations that have found their mark and cut so deep. They surge forward, grab him, drag him down the narrow streets, more and more people tailing along to see what is happening…then out one of the gates to an open waste area. He must be killed by ritual stoning. The heretic is to die outside the city walls, rejected by his people, just like his Master before him. The ringleaders get organized. "Come on everyone, collect stones." "Here, young Saul, look after our cloaks, we need our arms free for this." The brutal execution starts. First one, then another, then more and more stones find their mark.

Stephen, now on his knees, looks up. "Lord Jesus, I'm coming. You're ready for me, aren't you? Don't blame them for this." Then, mercifully, he's gone… the first of many in the Church who'll give their lives for the sake of Jesus and His great Purpose of rescuing a lost and rebellious race.

? DISCUSSION POINTS

1. In a church made up of members from a variety of ethnic backgrounds, what do you believe are some of the

    a) biggest challenges for those in leadership,

    b) potential advantages for that church as a whole, in contrast to a more culturally homogenous situation?

2. Think about examples of how God appointed and equipped different ones to lead His people in the earlier part of the Narrative. Can you identity any common threads that are coming out now in the emerging picture of leadership in the early Church?

3. It seems safe to assume that Stephen said the things he did to the Jewish leaders knowing they would react violently... even that he might be killed. How then would you explain his actions? Do you think he was illogical or reckless at all? Please explain. Can you apply your perspective about Stephen's choices to your own situation today?

2.15 Saul the persecutor becomes Saul the Apostle

 OBJECTIVES OF THIS TUTORIAL

This tutorial looks at the way Saul, a Jewish persecutor of the Church, was given a specific role in God's plans through a personal meeting with the Lord Jesus.
The portion of Scripture referred to in this tutorial is: **Acts 7:58, Acts chapters 8 and 9**

Last time
Luke's Narrative described a controversy that came up in the early Church between two groups with different cultural backgrounds. God's Spirit guided the Apostles to recognize a team of leaders - Deacons - within the group who would focus on practical service for the Church. This left the Apostles free to lead in other ways related directly to prayer and teaching God's Word. The Jewish authorities arrested one of the new leaders, Stephen. His speech inflamed their hatred further and they put him to death by ritual stoning.

Saul, a key player in Acts, comes on stage
Luke now focuses on an individual who, apart from God Himself, will prove to be the key player in the rest of the Acts account. A young man is watching the execution of Stephen with approval. He believes this new Jesus sect must be stamped out. There's no indication that he actually participates in the brutal killing himself, but he's associated with those who do and he's looking after their coats for them (Acts 7:58 and 8:1) Luke refers to him here early on by his Hebrew name, Saul, but later he'll go exclusively by Paul, which is the Roman equivalent. These two names - as we'll find out later in the Narrative - reflect the layers of Paul's identity and formative influences. A Roman citizen by birth, he is from a Jewish family that settled many years ago in the city of Tarsus - an important trade center on the Mediterranean coast of modern day Turkey. He's been indoctrinated into orthodox Pharisaical Judaism, but he's also had a classic Greek education perhaps including Stoic philosophy.

It's worth noting in passing here how God equips people, even before they know Him, for roles that He will later give them opportunity to take on. Paul, as we'll see, was incredibly well suited for the part God is about to offer to him in the outward reach of the Church. But for the moment, in Jerusalem, Saul is clearly considered by the orthodox Jewish leaders to be a young man with enormous potential.

The new Church suffers violent persecution

The events surrounding Stephen's death prove to be the initial earthquake that unleashes a tsunami of violent opposition against the Church (Acts 8:1-3). The Apostles stay put for now, but many of the believers leave Jerusalem to escape the tide of persecution...scattering to the outlying regions. Jesus had told the Apostles that they - His followers - were to be His witnesses first in Jerusalem, then in Judea and Samaria and to the world beyond. Now He's allowing circumstances to help them fulfill those instructions. Because, wherever they went, Luke records, they were sharing the Good News about Jesus. Here again we see God seamlessly weaving the smaller individual narratives of His image-bearers into His one Great Narrative.

Only a truly sovereign God could allow circumstances to affect His people without negating the genuine partnership He's eagerly seeking with them. As Jesus had clearly explained and modeled, participation in God's purpose of redeeming, or buying back, His lost race always involves cost.

The leaders of the Church in Jerusalem have already gladly accepted harassment, imprisonment, beating and, in Stephen's case, death, for the sake of their Lord. Now the rest of the group are having their commitment to Him and His Cause put to the test. Will they prioritize the reward of Jesus' loving approval that Stephen experienced so vividly at his death, or will they allow fear and even what many might call 'legitimate concerns' to shape their lives? It's a question that, in one form or another, God's Spirit poses to all those who claim to be Jesus' disciples... now just as much as then. Taking the lead in the persecution of the Church is the young zealous fundamentalist, Saul - he's determined to hunt down these followers of Jesus wherever they're holed up. This movement, this Jesus sect, must be stamped out once and for all. He's tireless in tracking them down and bringing them back to face punishment in Jerusalem.

The Gospel goes to Samaria and further afield

At this point in the Acts account (Acts 8:4-40), Luke takes a brief detour from following Saul's story to describe two incidents. They both involve one of the deacons from the Jerusalem church, Philip, who like many has been driven out of the city by the persecution after the death of his co-worker, Stephen. We won't take time to focus on Philip's experiences here, but they will prove to be very significant in the expansion of the

Church. The first finds Philip sharing the Good News in Samaria, with the result that a large number of people put their faith in Jesus as the Christ.

In the second incident, the Spirit of God gives Philip the opportunity to help a Jewish proselyte from Ethiopia understand that Jesus is the fulfillment of the Old Testament Narrative. The salvation of people from the theologically and ethnically aberrant Samaria, and now someone from an entirely non-Jewish people group, are important signposts of the ethnic inclusiveness inherent in the New Covenant.

Saul meets Jesus on the way to Damascus

But back to Saul... motivated by religious fervor and, no doubt, ambition, he gets authority from the High Priest to travel the 200 or so kilometers north to Damascus (Acts 9:1-3). Renowned as the oldest inhabited city in the world, it was the capital of the Roman province and modern day nation of Syria. It also seems to have been quite an active center for Jesus' followers in the early days as the Church is moving out from Jerusalem. And so Saul heads there with a group of armed men to hunt down as many as he can and drag them back to Jerusalem "in chains", the text says. Paul and his group are getting close to Damascus when the famous events unfold that lead to his conversion.

Suddenly, dramatically, the self-righteous assurance of this young man is shattered (Acts 9:3-9).

The Son of God, the Expression of the Creator in human form, the Word, in all the glory and authority of His existence in God's place as the Lamb-who-died-and-rose-again... Jesus, speaks His name, "Saul, Saul. Why are you persecuting me?" He says, *persecuting me*... although the oppression of His followers is effectively pushing them out into needy communities, just as Jesus intended, that doesn't mean He doesn't care about what they're going through. For Him, this is a very personal thing. What His Body experiences, impacts Him directly. No mistreatment of His blood-bought children goes unnoticed or, ultimately, unpunished.

The encounter with God's Son is a shattering blow to Saul's confident worldview assumptions... instead of doing things that will please God, as he thought, he's actually set himself up as the enemy of God. Blind, humbled, chastened by his encounter with Jesus, he is lead into Damascus... to wait for instructions, he's told. Lying in the darkness for the next three days, unable to eat or drink, he must be wondering what the future holds. He calls out to God, to His Son, to help him make sense of things...to tell him what to do next. What he doesn't know yet is that he's going to be given an amazing opportunity to serve the One he's been persecuting. While he's been hunting down the believers, God has been hunting him down. Now He's going to graciously give him a real purpose in life.

Ananias tells Saul about his new role

Luke introduces us to Ananias, a believer living in Damascus, who the Lord chooses to play a role in recruiting Saul to His global Cause (Acts 9:10-16). Ananias' appearance in the Narrative is very minor compared with the prominent part Saul will have, but that doesn't mean he contributes less or that his efforts are not just as valuable to the Lord. Much of the sacrifice and effort that's made for the Lord and His Church happen out of the limelight, with little or no public recognition. The encouragement to continue lies in the fact that the Master always notices and deeply appreciates the efforts of His people for Him and His Purpose.

Ananias is not exactly eager when the Lord tells him to go and speak on His behalf to Saul...*don't you know what a scary man this is, Lord?* But here's more evidence of God's commitment to involving His people in His purposes. As with Moses, the disciples, and many believers since, God's choice is not shaped by Ananias' own confidence or innate ability. In fact, as Saul himself will come to understand and articulate, God chooses ministry partners who are willing to rely on Him to overcome their own fear and shortcomings...because that way His power and wisdom is demonstrated most clearly. Although God does want us, His co-workers, to walk with Him by faith, even when we don't see the whole picture of what lies ahead, He isn't just after blind, mindless obedience. We've seen how Jesus, and now the Holy Spirit, work to draw faithful followers into a clear-eyed understanding of God's plans. So now He gives Ananias a glimpse of why it's so important that he puts aside his fears and goes to speak to Saul.

The Lord explains that He has chosen Saul to be one of His storytellers, His messengers. He'll have incredible opportunities to share the Message with his own Jewish people, but also to the non-Jewish ethnic groups, and to rulers. But as we've already noted, following the One who gave everything always costs the follower. Saul is also going to suffer for the sake of Jesus' name. Despite any lingering misgivings, Ananias gets up and goes to the house where God has told him that Saul is staying...on the road known as Via Recta or Straight Street in English that dissects the ancient city (Acts 9:17-19). It's still there today, mostly covered and part of a market in Damascus. Ananias introduces himself to his new brother in the faith, and Saul is immediately able to see again.

The former persecutor is persecuted

With his strength beginning to return, it's only a matter of days before Saul is going around to the local Jewish meeting places - their synagogues - trying to convince people that Jesus truly is the Son of God (Acts 9:20-30). Of course people are shocked to hear this from the young man, formerly the most orthodox of Jews and violently opposed to the Jesus sect.

Saul continues to learn from God's Spirit how to put forward powerful, convincing arguments from the Old Testament which, of course, he knows thoroughly from his studies under the Pharisees. The former enforcer for the orthodox Jewish authorities now becomes a target himself. Plans are made to murder him. They keep watch by the city gates to get him if he tries to leave. When this plot becomes known, a plan is devised to get Saul out… the same people he had come to the city to arrest now help him avoid capture by lowering him over the city wall in a large basket. Luke records that Saul makes his way back to Jerusalem. After some initial - and very understandable - suspicion on the part of the believers there, he's eventually introduced to the apostles and accepted as a brother in the faith. His very bold witness for Jesus in the capital results in an attempt on his life by the same Greek speaking, or Hellenized, Jews who'd played such a large part in Stephen's death. He leaves and heads off, probably by ship, to his hometown of Tarsus, the capital city in the Roman province of Cilicia.

Luke notes that these events mark a return to a time of peace for the Church, which now has a major presence in Jerusalem and surrounding provinces, in Galilee and in Samaria (Acts 9:31-32). Jesus' Plan for His Ecclesia to reach out from its initial small beginnings is moving forward. No longer isolated to one community, His Body, under the Spirit's guidance and encouragement is growing in numbers and spiritual strength where it is represented in different areas.

SAUL THE PERSECUTOR BECOMES SAUL THE APOSTLE

? DISCUSSION POINTS

1. Can you identify some ways that you believe God has equipped you, particularly in your formative years, for serving Him and His Church? If so, does that result at all in a sense of responsibility on your part to use your life in some specific way? If you could have a verbal conversation with Jesus about this issue, what do you think He might say to you?

2. What do you think about Jesus allowing persecution to come on His people to further His objectives? Do you feel that persecution would be a positive thing for your church to experience? Please explain. Is it legitimate to thank God, as is often done, for the freedom we have to meet openly without fear of reprisal?

2.16 The Lord sends Peter to teach the Gentiles

 OBJECTIVES OF THIS TUTORIAL

Jesus told Peter and the other Apostles that they were to be His witnesses not only in their local area but right out into the wider world. In this part of the Narrative, He makes it clear that He wants the Gentile nations to know Him and become part of His Church too.

The portion of Scripture referred to in this tutorial is: **Acts chapter 10**

Last time

We were introduced to Saul from the city of Tarsus, who will be the dominant character in the rest of the Acts Narrative. After Stephen's death, the young Church suffered a wave of violent persecution. Saul played a prominent role in the Jewish leaders' efforts to round up and punish Jesus' followers. On his way to Damascus to hunt down believers, Saul was suddenly knocked over and temporarily blinded when Jesus revealed Himself in His glory to him. Later, God sent His servant Ananias to explain to Saul that he had been chosen to play an enormously important role in the expansion of the Church. Saul quickly made enemies among the Jews in Damascus then Jerusalem when He began to testify that Jesus was, indeed, the Son of God.

Gentiles in the Church? A question no one is asking

God is about to take His *Ecclesia* - His *called-out people* - into completely new territory... not so much, this time, into new *geographical* areas, but rather into uncharted realms of ethnicity and identity. It will launch His Church on a journey into new language and culture frontiers, which continues today. As always though, following Jesus further into His purpose will cost. But this time the obstacles won't come from antagonistic authorities, and the pain won't be the kind that results from a beating. In fact, what they face is for them, and us, a much more daunting and painful kind of challenge - when God's Spirit shows us how our most cherished assumptions are wrong, and that they need to be changed.

Up to this point, everyone who has put their faith in Jesus as Messiah - and subsequently had God's Spirit come to join them to His Church - has been a Jew. Yes, the Samaritans have dubious theological credentials but they do at least follow the Law of Moses...they respect the Sabbath, and practice the rituals and sacrifice for their sins. And most importantly, the men - the leaders of the families and communities - have the permanent sign of being God's people on their bodies... they are circumcised. Oh, there was that government official from Ethiopia that believed and was baptized into the faith by Phillip, but he was a practicing Jew as well. That's why he had come all the way to Jerusalem and was reading the words of the prophet Isaiah. As a foreign convert he'd have gone through all the necessary rituals for proselytes and would, of course, be circumcised.

Certainly no one's thinking that non-Jews - the uncircumcised Gentiles - can just believe in Jesus as Saviour and be joined to the *Ecclesia*. Of course not! It goes without saying that for someone to come under the New Covenant, they must first have to comply with the Old Covenant. You can't just become a follower of Jesus and have God's Spirit enter if you haven't first become one of God's people, under Moses' Law. That would be ridiculous! What, you mean like Phoenician sailors or Cretans or Assyrians or... those Romans, being added to the Church? I don't think so. No, no, God isn't going to let that happen!

An angel speaks to the Roman captain, Cornelius

Now, in his Account, Luke introduces us to one of those very Romans (Acts 10:1-8). Kornēlios (or Cornelius in English), was a non-commissioned officer ...a captain commanding a company of soldiers recruited in Italy. They are stationed with the rest of their brigade in the city of Caesarea on the Mediterranean coast, about 100 kilometers northwest of Jerusalem. We aren't told how it came about, but Cornelius and his family have turned from the polytheism and Emperor cult practices of their Roman culture to worship the one, true Creator God. He hasn't gone through circumcision and the rest of the process to become a Jewish proselyte but he is devoutly religious...he's generous to needy people in the community and is disciplined in his prayers to God.

In fact, it's while Cornelius is praying one afternoon that God sends one of His angels with a message. Yet again we're going to see how God the Author continues to write His Narrative in real events and in the lives of human beings. The threads of what is about to unfold here connect back to promises God made to Abraham when He'd said that through him He'd bless all the ethnic groups - the *nations* - of the earth. The angel messenger gives very specific instructions to a rather stunned and terrified Cornelius: He's to send for a guy called Simon Peter who's in the ancient seaport of Joppa (today a suburb of Tel Aviv). He's staying there in the house of a man called Simon, who tans animal hides for a living. They'll find his house right by the ocean, which is what you'd expect, because seawater is used in the traditional curing process.

We've noted many times before from His Narrative that God is eager to reveal Himself to human beings, and when they respond to that revelation He offers them even more. This is the case with Cornelius. He has been relating humbly to God in light of what he knows so far... but religious devotion won't bring him into the relationship with God that he's seeking. There is still a great deal he needs to understand, and God is giving him the opportunity to find that out. Cornelius immediately responds to the offer - he sends some trusted men to find this Peter that the angel has told him about.

God challenges Peter's assumptions

They travel south down the coast and the next day around midday they're nearing the end of their 50 kilometer trip (Acts 10:9-20). What they don't know is that the guy they're looking for in Joppa - who of course is the Apostle Peter - is himself about to have some amazing things revealed to him by God. He's up on the typically flat roof of the house, perhaps to get an ocean breeze and escape the all-pervasive smell coming from the tanning process below. An orthodox Jew would shun this place and these people because of the ritual uncleanness associated with dead animals. Peter has been willing to come here, probably because Simon and others there are believers, but it's likely that he's been pondering the whole issue of 'clean' and 'unclean' and what that means under the New Covenant. He's also hungry, and while he's waiting for a meal to be prepared in the house the thought of food is no doubt on his mind. God's Spirit uses these very real, very relevant circumstances as the context in which to teach Peter something with profound implications.

While he's there thinking and praying, his awareness of the house, the ocean and other things around him fade... he's seeing something being let down from the sky, a big piece of material maybe. It's an astonishing sight. In this large sheet are "all sorts of animals, reptiles, and birds" the text records. But then, shockingly, a voice tells him to kill and eat them. We don't know if it's Jesus' voice he recognizes but he answers Him as *Lord*. And, characteristically, he protests vigorously - Oh no, he couldn't ever eat something like that! He's always followed the Jewish dietary laws and has never eaten what Moses' law prohibits - animals like camels, pigs and hares, birds like eagles, and most certainly no reptiles! And even the animals that are meant to be eaten are all mixed in with the others, so they are now 'unclean' as well.

The Lord challenges him. Who is Peter to call something unclean that God is now telling him is okay, to reject what He accepts? Three times this whole thing is repeated... it's not his imagination, God is insisting, pressing the point home. But even now he's not fully clear about all the implications. Is it just about dietary laws or are there wider implications in what God has shown him? As always, God's timing is perfect. His Spirit, who is always with Peter, ready to point him in the right direction if he's listening, tells him that he's to go with the three men who've just arrived at the door.

Peter adjusts his thinking and behavior

Clearly God's truth has begun to significantly reshape Peter's worldview assumptions, his beliefs and values, and is impacting his behavior. (Acts 10:21-43) He invites the Gentile visitors to stay for the night - something no orthodox Jew would do - and then the next day he happily travels with them to the house of a Roman officer. As Peter explains when they arrive in Caesarea, entering the house of a Gentile or hanging out with them is against the Jewish law... but God has made it clear that old categories based on ethnicity are invalid. God doesn't value one race over another. And now the former fisherman shares with this Gentile family the Good News that has, so far, only been made available to the Jews.

Cornelius and his family already worship the one true God. They know they are sinners and need His forgiveness and salvation. They know something of what the prophets have foretold about the Messiah. Clearly from what Peter says they are also familiar with the story of Jesus of Nazareth, and even realize that He was someone sent by God to do good. They've heard that He was crucified. But then, with the unshakable assurance of an eyewitness, Peter also tells them that God brought Jesus back to life. He and the other Apostles had spent time - even eating and drinking - with Him after His resurrection. Peter concludes by clearly describing the choice they have: they can choose to face Jesus as God's holy, appointed judge, or turn to Him in faith as the promised Redeemer and have their sins forgiven.

Cornelius' family saved and part of the Church

The truth of all this is resonating with Cornelius, his family, and the people who are part of their household (Acts 10:44-48). There's no record of a particular formula or words they're told to pray - they simply believe everything Peter is saying as truth from God. And in that moment, seeing their faith, God rescues them from the control of Satan and their past identity as Adam's descendants; He wipes out their sin-debt and places them into His family, as righteous and cherished as His Son. And, under the New Covenant, they are now part of His Gathering, His Church. No application form is filled out, and no ritual takes place... they are miraculously joined into the Body by God's Spirit who now comes to live in them permanently.

Peter has brought some other Jewish believers along and they are amazed by what they're seeing and hearing. These are Romans, Gentiles! They don't sacrifice at the Temple in Jerusalem, they probably eat whatever they like, run around on the Sabbath...

and they're not even circumcised! But look at them now. They're praising God for His Son Jesus… and now they're speaking in other languages that they've never learnt. God has poured out His Spirit on these guys just like He did for us on the day of Pentecost. Obviously the New Covenant of Jesus' blood is also for those who've never even been under the Old Covenant. Wow, this changes everything. So that's what Jesus meant, Peter, when He told you and the other Apostles that we were to be His witnesses not only in this area but right out into the world. He wants the Gentile nations to know Him and become part of His *Ecclesia* too! Peter agrees and Cornelius and the others are baptized so they can demonstrate in an outward, physical, way what has already taken place spiritually inside.

THE LORD SENDS PETER TO TEACH THE GENTILES

? DISCUSSION POINTS

1. Can you think of an example of some worldview assumptions you've held but which you then realized God was challenging - directly through His word, through events, or through someone else?

2. Imagine you've been sharing the Narrative up to this point with a friend who's had no other exposure to the Bible. How would you respond if one day they said they'd been talking with a Christian who regularly gets instructions from God speaking directly to them and sometimes in visions from angels?

3. Do you think that Peter would have felt free to eat some pork if he was offered it in Cornelius' house? Drawing only from what you think Peter would know up to this point, explain your answer.

4. Based on this event in the Narrative and all we've learned so far, do you believe there is evidence to say that someone needs to pray something in order to be saved? Please explain.

➡ ACTIVITIES

1. In just a few sentences for each, describe Caesarea and Joppa respectively, providing whatever details you feel are helpful in understanding the Acts account. Include a map and an image or two if you like.

2.17 The Church moves outward

> **OBJECTIVES OF THIS TUTORIAL**
>
> The continuing Narrative in Acts tells of an exciting period of expansion of the Church, as the believers take the message of Truth with them to a wider group of Gentile communities. It shows the complexities and challenges for individuals involved in the process, but also the clear guidance and hand of the Lord in preparing the way.
> The portion of Scripture referred to in this tutorial is: **Acts chapters 11 and 12**

Last time

We were introduced to a Roman officer, Cornelius, who believed in the God of Israel but had not gone through the process of formally becoming a Jew. On receiving instructions from God, Cornelius sent some men to another city to find Peter. Just as the men were approaching, God was dramatically challenging Peter about how he, like others, had wrongly brought Old Covenant, Jewish perspectives into the new era of Christ's Church. With his perspective changed, Peter gladly went to Cornelius' house and shared the Gospel with them. They put their faith in Jesus, were born again, and clearly were given the gift of the Holy Spirit by God.

The way was now open for the Church to reach out to other ethnic groups knowing that God wanted to include them under the New Covenant as well.

Peter responds to criticism

The news about what happened in Caesarea doesn't take long to get back to the other Apostles and the believers in the Jerusalem area (Acts 11:1-18). You might think that their response would be total excitement that God was also bringing Gentiles into the *Ecclesia*. But that isn't the case, or at least not for the believers who've come from an orthodox Jewish background. We'll see that this conservative faction in the early Church will continue to cause problems and jeopardize the clarity and freedom of the Gospel by trying to impose Jewish traditions on the Church.

Like all of us, they have deep-seated worldview beliefs and values that need to be re-evaluated in light of God's Narrative - all that He has done and is doing. They need the Spirit's help to put aside assumptions and prejudices so they can have a clearer view of who He is and how He is accomplishing His purposes at this particular time in history.

So when Peter arrives back in Jerusalem, still excited no doubt from what he's been part of, he's immediately faced with criticism. No one seems to have a problem with him sharing the Good News about Jesus with Gentiles or wants to argue about the Spirit coming to live in non-Jews. As is usually the case with people who struggle to grasp God's grace, their disapproval focuses on outward, peripheral things. Peter, we heard that you went into the home of Gentiles… and even ate with them! What were you thinking? Are you forgetting the traditions of our people, God's people, the Jews? And you a leader! What kind of example is that for others? We have to maintain standards… Or words to that effect.

You've got to wonder how the old Peter would have responded. But guided by God's Spirit who's always with him now, Peter doesn't jump to his own defense. What he does is simply describe in detail the things that God has revealed and allowed him to participate in. Luke records that when the others have heard Peter's account of what happened in Joppa and then Caesarea, "they stopped objecting and began praising God". At least for now, even those wanting the Church to hold on to Jewish traditions have had their eyes raised above the horizon of their narrow agendas and prejudice… they've glimpsed the fact that God is doing something far beyond the restrictions they try to impose on themselves, on others, and even on Him.

The Gospel impacts Gentiles in Antioch

Luke continues on (Acts 11:19-21) to describe how the Lord is giving the believers opportunities to share His Truth with non-Jewish ethnic groups in increasingly wider contexts. He refers to the believers who scattered during the time of fierce persecution after the death of Stephen… the violent harassment and arrests in which the young Pharisee, Saul, played a prominent role before Jesus stopped him, quite literally, in his tracks.

Fleeing the heat of opposition, some have gone north to the strip of Mediterranean coast then called *Phoenicia*, in modern day Lebanon. Some had shipped out to Cyprus - the island about 100 kilometers off the coast of both Turkey and Syria. Others have traveled up to Antioch in Syria (called that, to distinguish it from 15 other cities called *Antioch* at this time). Located near the northeastern corner of the Mediterranean, it is the third largest city in the Roman Empire and the western end of the Silk Road that stretches all the way east to the mysterious land we know today as China.

These believers are *Hellenists,* i.e. influenced by Greek, and then Roman, language and culture. They are sharing the Good News that the Messiah has come in these places with other Hellenist Jews. But now the pattern is challenged. Some of those who escape to Antioch are from families who settled generations before on the island of Cyprus and also in Cyrene, a port city in North Africa, now part of the Roman Empire. Incidentally, we'll remember that this was the home town of Simon who carried Jesus' cross on the way to Golgotha. Having grown up in communities outside Israel, these believers are linguistically and culturally more open. They begin to share the Good News with people in Antioch who are not from a Jewish background. God blesses their witness and a large number of people put their faith in Jesus as the Saviour. The church in that city grows rapidly and in many ways, as we'll see, takes over from Jerusalem as the center of its outward thrust. The *Ecclesia* has taken another significant step in the task of expansion given by Jesus.

The Apostles send Barnabas to Antioch

At this point Luke reintroduces someone who'll play a significant role in the Acts part of the Narrative - Barnabas (Acts 11:22-24). He mentioned him first as a prime example of the generosity that characterized the early Church in Jerusalem (Acts 4:36-37), then again as the one who courageously introduced the newly converted Saul to the Apostles when the rest of the believers were suspicious (Acts 9:27). His Jewish name is in fact Joseph, but he's nick-named Barnabas by the Apostles... a Greek word that means "encourager" because that's what this godly, faithful man is known for among the believers.

When the Apostles in Jerusalem hear about the rapid growth in the Antioch gathering, they send their trusted co-worker Barnabas to verify if things are actually on track. Himself from a Hellenized Jewish background in Cyprus, he is a good choice to send to the ethnically diverse milieu that is Antioch. We don't see any evidence of the Apostles creating a hierarchy to rule over the groups of believers appearing in different places now. Under the New Covenant the pattern is one of service to each other rather than a ruling elite. But we do see the Apostles functioning in Jesus' authority and taking responsibility for the integrity of the Good News about Him as it is being shared in new contexts. Also demonstrating a concern that whatever is claimed as part of His *Ecclesia* - His Body - clearly has the hallmarks of the Spirit's involvement. Barnabas finds in Antioch what the Apostles had hoped he would - evidence that God is indeed at work here. He jumps in and gets involved... God uses him to bring even more people to faith in Jesus as the Saviour.

Barnabas brings Saul to Antioch

With so much need and opportunity, Barnabas remembers the young Pharisee scholar, Saul, who'd led the persecution of the believers after Stephen's death... the one who'd met Jesus on the road to Damascus and been so dramatically changed. What an asset he would be to the work here in Antioch! With his knowledge of the Old Covenant Scriptures and understanding of Jewish traditions, he'd be a powerful witness to the Jews. Having grown up in the Hellenistic environment of Tarsus and being trained in classical Greek logic, he'd also be able to put forward convincing arguments to the Gentiles. And that time in Jerusalem after his conversion he'd shown such courage and commitment to the cause of the Lord Jesus. All he needs is someone to give him some encouragement and direction. So Barnabas sets out to find Saul in his home town of Tarsus, over 200 kilometers away around the bend of the Mediterranean - today a three-hour drive, it no doubt took Barnabas some days of tough travel to get there (Acts 11:25,26).

The Story of the expansion of the early Church is certainly one of dramatic events, of sermons, and miracles, that result in large numbers being converted. But it also describes another quieter but no less powerful contribution: faithful followers of Jesus reaching out to others who are younger or newer in the Faith… seeing their potential, believing in them, carefully equipping and gently guiding, including them in God's purposes, then gratefully working alongside them as co-workers.

Barnabas finds Saul in Tarsus and brings him back to Antioch where they work together in the local group of Jesus' followers - His Church - in that city. They have great opportunities to share the Gospel with many people. Luke mentions in passing that it is here that the believers are first called *Christians* or *Christ followers*… a term probably used by others in mockery.

A famine looms in Judea and elsewhere

Luke describes how some believers come from Jerusalem to Antioch and, with special insights from the Holy Spirit, prophesy that a major famine is coming (Acts 11:27-30). History records that this series of famines hit many parts of the Roman Empire during the reign of the Emperor Claudius. This helps to place the founding of the Antioch church around A.D. 40, possibly 10 to 15 years after Jesus' death and resurrection. Understanding that the famine will be particularly harsh in Judea, the believers in Antioch collect gifts and have Barnabas and Saul deliver this practical help to their brothers and sisters in the Jerusalem church.

James is executed but Peter goes free

While the Judean believers are dealing with the shortages and hunger of the famine, they have to face renewed persecution (Acts 12:1-17). This time it comes from King Herod Agrippa… grandson of Herod the Great. Like other vassal kings at the time, he depends on the favor of Rome. It will put him in a good light to inflate the idea of a threat from this 'Jewish sect' of Jesus followers by violently suppressing them. He executes James - the first Apostle to be martyred and the only one directly included in the Acts account.

Herod realizes that his brutality against the Christian leader has also bought him plaudits from the Jewish authorities… their support is important in the delicate political balancing act he has to play as their territorial king under Roman rule. So during Passover, when the most publicity is assured, he arrests Peter, the recognized leader of the Jesus followers in Jerusalem. But even Herod knows it will be going too far to murder Peter during Passover, so he's put in prison to await trial and inevitable execution. The believers are praying constantly. Their dear brother James is gone, but that must have been the Master's will. If He chooses, He can graciously rescue Peter. Nothing is too difficult for Him. From ancient times He's shown that He can rescue His people.

It's the middle of the night before the trial… Peter is asleep, chained between two soldiers. He feels something hitting his side. What is that? Must be one of the guards turning in his sleep? No, something else. Who's that, someone leaning over telling me to get up? How did I get on my feet…and hey, aren't those my chains lying on the floor, still attached to the guards? Who is that, urging me to get dressed and follow? I can't see too well in this strange bright light flooding the cell. It has to be an angel. This must be a dream, or a vision… I've had those before once or twice when the Lord has spoken to me. No doubt I'll wake up still in chains. Well, nothing to do but go with the flow, follow along. We're out of the cell… here's the first guard post, and there's the second. Why don't they notice anything, sound the alarm? The big iron gates are opening ahead of us… we're outside in the cool air.

Suddenly in the quiet city streets, the angel is gone and Peter is alone. And finally he knows for sure… it's no dream, it's real. God has rescued him from certain execution at the hands of Herod and the Jewish leaders. He realizes he'd better get off the streets. He heads to the house of a believer, a lady named Mary, whose house is used as a gathering place for the church in Jerusalem. Her son, John Mark, is the Mark who we understand wrote the Gospel account of Jesus' life. As it happens, the believers are gathered in Mary's house praying for Peter's release. There is a moment of comical confusion before everyone believes that it is actually their much loved brother and Apostle who's knocking on the door outside waiting to be let in. Before Peter leaves again, he asks the believers to share what has happened with James and the other Apostles - this James is the half brother of the Lord Jesus who by now is one of the leaders in the Jerusalem church.

THE CHURCH MOVES OUTWARD

❓ DISCUSSION POINTS

1. What lesson or principle do you think there is to learn from the way that the Spirit guided Peter to handle the critical attitude of the Jewish traditionalist believers when he came back to Jerusalem?

2. Thinking "Narratively", reflect on any links you can see between how God consistently seeks to work with faithful people and how Barnabas related to Saul (first in Jerusalem and then in bringing him to Antioch)?

3. What would you say to someone, hearing this part of the Acts account for the first time, who was troubled by the fact that the Lord allowed James to be executed but chose to rescue Peter?

4. What part do you think the prayers of the Jerusalem believers played in Peter being released, in contrast to James being killed? Did it come down to factors like how many prayed, for how long, and with what degree of faith? Or none of these? How does your perspective on this impact your view and practice of prayer?

➡ ACTIVITIES

1. In approximately half a page, note what you consider to be the five most important landmark events in the expansion of the Church so far in the Acts Narrative. Include a brief explanation for each as to why it is so significant.

2.18 The Church sends out Paul & Barnabas

✓ OBJECTIVES OF THIS TUTORIAL

In what is commonly described as Paul's first missionary journey, the book of Acts now describes the effort by the Church to reach out beyond its borders to the ends of the earth, by sending Barnabas and Paul on a journey to share God's Word. They ask John Mark to join them.

The portion of Scripture referred to in this tutorial is: **Acts 13:1-43**

Last time

Peter responded to the criticism from the Jewish traditionalists for going and eating in the house of the Gentile, Cornelius, by simply giving a report of all that God had done during that time.

Hellenist believers from Cyprus, who'd fled the previous persecution in Jerusalem, went to Antioch in Syria and shared the Good News with Gentiles there. Many were saved and added to the Church. Barnabas, sent by the Apostles to assess this rapid growth, found that God's Spirit indeed was at work. He went to Tarsus and brought Saul back to help with the many opportunities to witness in Antioch.

King Herod Agrippa, executed the Apostle James, but when he arrested Peter in order to also have him killed, God miraculously rescued the former fisherman from prison.

The Antioch church is led by a diverse, gifted team

Over the last fifteen years or so since Jesus returned to a place of honor and authority beside His Father, the Apostles and early believers have been obeying His instructions to go out with the Good News about Him... to teach truth and make disciples in Jerusalem, Judea and Samaria. Since Pentecost, the Gospel has gained a foothold in a significant number of communities around the eastern end of the Mediterranean. But now the time has come for the Church to make a more concerted push out towards the "ends of the earth".

Significantly, the initiative comes from God's Spirit. All efforts to further the Church's task that have proven to be effective - both in the time of the Apostles and down through history - have been directed and empowered by God. Luke tells of a particular day when the leaders of the Antioch church are gathered together, their thoughts focused on the Lord Jesus (Acts 13:1).

It's worth noting some features of this leadership team from Luke's description, because it fits with a pattern that will emerge more fully in the ongoing Narrative. First of all, they are functioning together as a group of committed co-workers with no indication of a hierarchy. Secondly, they are a culturally diverse group with no ethnicity being elevated over any other. Thirdly, we're told that the Antioch leadership team is comprised of both *prophets* and *teachers*.

Distinction made between *prophecy* and *teaching*

The distinction in these roles or *gifts* is important to understand in light of the pivotal transition that is still taking place during the period described here in Acts. For 400 years, as the Old Covenant wound down, God had not appointed any new storytellers or *prophets* to add to His revelation - His Narrative. Now that the New Covenant has been instituted through Jesus' death and resurrection, His Spirit is giving specific individuals within the *Ecclesia* the role and ability to speak for Him...to reinterpret the existing Narrative in light of what Jesus has accomplished and to instruct His children how to live in this new era - as individuals and as local *ecclesia*. All of the Apostles are designated *prophets*, but there are many others in the early Church who are given the privilege of being channels for God's special revelation during this transitional period. In time, as the revelation is written down and consolidates into what we know as the New Testament, the need for this role diminishes and eventually disappears.

The gift of *teaching* is identified as distinct from *prophecy*, although some, like the Apostles, are gifted with both roles. The responsibility of teaching is all about taking the *prophecy* - God's special or new revelation - and making it clear among the churches, such as in Antioch, so it can be applied in real life situations that the believers are facing. The need for this *gift* continues beyond the transitional Acts era, and nearly 2000 years later we can be grateful that wherever the true Church can be found, the Spirit still gives certain men the capacity to clarify and apply the words of the Old and New Covenant prophets contained in the Bible.

Antioch church sends out a church planting team

But back to Luke's record (Acts 13:2,3), God's Spirit makes it clear, no doubt through one of His prophet spokesmen there, that they are to appoint Saul and Barnabas to undertake some special work that He has for them. Losing these two gifted and committed members of their team, even for a time, must certainly have represented a sacrifice for the others, but they obviously have a perspective that reaches beyond the needs of their church and immediate community. There is a clear sense of the church's investment in this venture, as they send the pair out to take part in the Lord's global purposes.

And so begins the first of what have become known as *Paul's missionary journeys*. Very soon, either by his own choice, as he moves away from his former Jewish identity, or through author Luke's read of the situation, the former Pharisee scholar from Tarsus will be known in the Narrative by the Latin version of his name, Paul. He and Barnabas take young John Mark with them - who we find out later in the Narrative is a cousin of Barnabas. Also, as we've noted before, there's very strong evidence that this is the same Mark who wrote the account of Jesus' life that we know as the second Gospel.

Another pattern is established here that we'll see repeated throughout the Acts Narrative. Even though Paul obviously has a very prominent role, the early Church's efforts to take the truth into new areas actually takes place through a network of inter-dependent teams, with the support of local churches… a very different picture from the over-achieving super-gifted individualist missionary that's sometimes projected as the ideal. Involving younger co-worker disciples like John Mark is something we've already seen Barnabas do, and we'll likewise see Paul make a habit of doing this with others.

Barnabas, Paul and John Mark go to Cyprus

With God's Spirit guiding them, they head first to Barnabas' home island of Cyprus. That probably meant a couple of hours' walk from Antioch down to the harbor at Seleucia, then on board one of the square-rigged cargo ships that reserve some space for passengers (the picture below is of a replica of a Roman '*corbita*' thought to be the type used by Paul). With good weather and favorable winds, they'd be docking in Salamis, the main port on the island's east coast, before nightfall (Acts 13:4-12).

Luke doesn't say specifically, but it's very possible they were welcomed here by a small *ecclesia* in this city that is the main commercial center for the island. If so, the church is made up of believers who fled the persecution a few years ago in Jerusalem and others who've been reached through their witness for the Lord Jesus. While in town, Paul, Barnabas and John Mark visit the Jewish synagogue and preach God's Word - something that will be a pattern in many places they visit on their travels.

After leaving Salamis, they travel "from town to town across the entire island" as the text puts it. Along the way they have opportunity to share the truth with the governor of the island, who becomes a believer. Although the Narrative doesn't say specifically, this conversion of a well-educated Roman aristocrat may have been a pivotal point for

Paul in shaping and broadening his view of who God intends for him to target with the proclamation of the Good News.

John Mark leaves; Paul and Barnabas go to Antioch

The three men leave Cyprus by ship from *Paphos* on the southwest coast, headed for *Pamphylia*, a region in the south of the area known then as *Asia Minor* - today part of the Antalya province in Turkey (Acts 13:13-43). They land in *Perga*, coastal gateway to the area and a city known for malaria. Later Paul will mention that he was sick soon after having gone through there. At this point, John Mark leaves them and heads back to Jerusalem. Luke doesn't comment here on the dynamics, but we find out later in the Narrative that Paul isn't impressed and considers it a desertion...it will be a long time before his trust in the younger man is restored. Meanwhile, Paul and Barnabas head north over very rugged terrain on roads notorious for bandits. They reach the Roman colony city Antioch... often distinguished from other cities with the same name by referencing the nearby region of *Pisidia*. Luke records that the two men attend the Sabbath service at the local synagogue and Paul accepts an invitation to speak. He skillfully ties together threads from the Old Covenant Narrative, focusing first of all on God's sovereignty and His grace. Then he asserts clearly that God has made a way through the death and resurrection of King David's descendant, Jesus, for people to have their sins forgiven and to stand righteous in His eyes - something the Law given to Moses could never achieve. He strongly urges his audience to listen and believe this message from God.

We should note that it's not only ethnic Jews who hear the Good News proclaimed in the synagogues they visit in this city and elsewhere. The Jewish diaspora in the period of Hellenisation two or three centuries before, means that many communities throughout much of the Roman Empire have been exposed to the truth about the one Creator God. Some have converted to Judaism, submitting to the initiation rituals - most notably circumcision. Many others, while believing in the God of the Jews, are not prepared to take such a definitive step... but they do attend the synagogue regularly to hear teaching from the ancient Jewish Scriptures. In these cases, they are inevitably familiar with the passages foretelling the coming of the Messiah from the prophets, such as Isaiah. As we'll see from the Narrative, Paul and the others often find soil already well prepared for the Good News among these Gentile worshippers. In fact, a number of them will end up being the core of local fellowships that spring up in many of the cities Paul and the others visit. By contrast, it is often the orthodox Jews who react negatively and even violently to this new revelation from God and those who bring it.

❓ DISCUSSION POINTS

1. To what degree do you feel that we should interpret the circumstances and events described in the Acts account as transitional? Please elaborate on your answer. Try to avoid as much as possible existing labels or doctrinal positions…think in terms of how you see God's Narrative leading us to place this time of the Apostles within the whole picture of His revelation and purposes.

2. What does the term missionary represent:

a) for you,

b) for other Christians you know,

c) for non-Christians in general?

On the whole, do you feel it is a positive thing to have this special designation? Why? If you were sent out from your church to work in another culture, how would you like to be described?

 ACTIVITIES

1. Look closely at Paul's sermon in the synagogue (Acts 13:16-41). Then:

a) Provide tentative section headings if we were to divide it up like this: vv16-25, vv26-37 and vv38-41.

b) Make any observations you can about the way he tailored his message for his audience.

c) Identify any lessons you've learned from his example to help in sharing the Gospel with others?

2.19 Paul's teaching journey continues

 OBJECTIVES OF THIS TUTORIAL

The Narrative now describes the continuing journey of Paul and Barnabas. They teach God's Word clearly in a number of cities, encountering both violent opposition and also those who listen to their message.
The portion of Scripture referred to in this tutorial is: **Acts 13:44-14:27**

Last time

We noted that the Antioch church was led by a group of ethnically diverse leaders, equipped by God for their roles. Paul and Barnabas were sent out by the church to take the Good News to communities where it was not yet accessible. They took John Mark and traveled in Cyprus before heading to Perga in the area known as Asia Minor. After John Mark left them they headed north to the city of Antioch in Pisidia where they had opportunity to share the Gospel in the local synagogue.

Paul and Barnabas target the Gentiles

Paul's sermon in the Pisidian Antioch synagogue generates a great deal of interest and he's given opportunity to share again the next week. This time, Luke says, "almost the entire city" turns up to hear (Acts 13:44-49). But some of the Jews don't like all this attention the two visitors are getting and they begin to publicly argue with them. This brings a strong reaction from God's two spokesmen, and they make a dramatic declaration with implications that will echo out around the world and down through the centuries to us.

Certainly the life-bringing Word has to be offered first to the Jews - they are, after all, God's original Covenant people. It was to them the written Narrative had originally been given, and Jesus the Messiah had been born to a woman of that race. Also, as God stated through the prophet Isaiah (Isaiah 49:6) centuries before, it was them as a people who He'd first tasked with being a light that would draw all the ethnic groups throughout the world to Him and provide them access to His salvation. But now that the Messiah has come and the Way has been made clear, the Jews have rejected that very way of salvation. So, the Good News is going to be offered to the Gentiles. Another implication of all this - although not explicated in the Narrative at this point - is that the privilege of being God's light- and salvation-bearers to the world's ethnic groups will now also be handed over to His New Covenant people.

The God-fearing Gentiles in the crowd are, understandably, excited by this announcement that God's grace and salvation through Jesus is not limited to a Jewish ethnic identity. Luke makes an editorial comment that it is very much in line with God's purposes that these Gentiles who gratefully believe the Good News will receive eternal life. Their inclusion as non-Jews into God's family is not something they or Paul and Barnabas have orchestrated; it is the result of God's sovereign, gracious choice. Their effort to share the Gospel among the Gentiles results in many coming to faith throughout the whole area.

They move on and plant a church in Iconium

The Jews, of course, are outraged by anything that questions their assumptions of a privileged place in God's plans....they use their influence with the city leaders to stir up trouble and have Paul and Barnabas run out of town (Acts 13:50-14:3). Luke records that the two shake the dust of that city off their shoes as they're moving on. There's an irony involved here, as this symbolic gesture was something pious Jews were in the habit of doing as they left Gentile cities to symbolize a complete rejection of the heathen ways. It also seems likely Paul and Barnabas had heard Jesus' disciples recount how when He was sending them out on their first witnessing assignment, He'd said they should shake the dust off their feet if they were rejected by a household or community.

The experience of being evicted from the town doesn't make them lose heart or come to the conclusion that they are not 'called' to this kind of work after all. For one thing, they know that they've contributed to the existence of a group of new believers who are excited about their faith and are being guided by the Holy Spirit who is now living in them. No doubt too, Paul and Barnabas remind themselves that it was God Himself who'd told them and their fellow leaders back in Syrian Antioch to initiate this effort they are spearheading. They also clearly have a growing comprehension of how God is reaching out to the different people groups at this time, and a sense of the part He wants them to play. And finally, as Paul will later explain in letters he writes to believers in different places, it is the love of the Lord Jesus Himself that he feels propelling him forward into new areas with the Good News.

So they head east and south about 100 kilometers to Iconium, site of today's Turkish city of Konya - traveling, we can assume, along the well-made Roman road that joined the two cities. Here the same thing happens as in the last place...Paul and Barnabas go to the synagogue and proclaim God's truth. It's worth noting that despite their previous strong statements about God opening the door to the Gentile nations in the face of Jewish national rejection of their Messiah, it does not mean He is no longer reaching out to the Jews as individuals. Luke doesn't give details, but the way the two travelers share the Gospel is extremely effective and a large number of both Jews and Gentiles come to faith in Jesus.

But just like in the previous city, it is some of the die-hard traditionalist Jews who reject the message and stir up trouble for the two church planters. Rather than direct open antagonism, this time Satan uses one of his favorite tactics - he encourages self-righteous religious people to indulge in poisonous slander and gossip against those who are sharing the truth that they find uncomfortable. Despite the controversy their message is creating and the opposition they're personally facing, Paul and Barnabas decide they're not walking away. They stay a long time - probably some months - "preaching boldly about the grace of the Lord" as the text records. To counteract the lies that are being told and to authenticate their message, the Lord gives them the ability to do what is described as "miraculous signs and wonders". With no authoritative New Covenant Narrative yet written to base their teaching on, these supernatural evidences of the Spirit's involvement were crucial in the early outreaches of the Church.

They travel to a different church planting context

The Gospel message, with its exclusive claims about Jesus Christ, is inherently controversial. When Jesus' messengers - then or now - are being guided by His Spirit they are, like Him, full of grace...they gladly reach out with love and empathy to those around them. But also like Him, they share His message in such a way that people have to either accept or reject Him. And that's the way it is in Iconium - the people are polarized. Eventually those opposing the Christian message win the upper hand and with the blessing of the city leaders they plan to attack Paul and Barnabas and kill them with stones (Acts 14:4-18). But the two hear about the plot and decide it's a wise time to leave and take the Good News to another community. They head southwest, to the town of Lystra on the eastern part of the high, rather barren plains of the Lycaonia region.

In covering the 30 or so kilometers between Iconium and Lystra, the two church planters have crossed an important frontier. Although as a Roman colony Latin is the official language, they are hearing Lycaonian being spoken around them...a dialect they can't understand. This minority language will actually survive for another 500 years before being overtaken by Greek. At this point, Paul and Barnabas are not much more than a day's walk from the limits of the Roman Empire proper. Just as Jesus had commanded some 20 or so years before, His *Body*, His *Ecclesia*, is reaching out with His Good News into the more far-flung ethnic groups.

Also different, is the fact that this is the first town they visit on the entire trip in which there's no mention of a synagogue. Educated Greek philosophy or Jewish monotheism have made little impact, and the prevailing worldview is a blend of Greek mythology and local cultish practices. These beliefs condition the people's response when they observe Paul being used to miraculously heal a physically handicapped man. Because of the language and culture barriers, the two visiting church planters don't understand at first that they are being hailed by the locals as gods. When it becomes apparent that elaborate preparations are being made to offer sacrifices to them, Paul and Barnabas protest in the strongest possible terms. They try to convince the people that they are only human beings who've come with a message from the living God.

In contrast to previous contexts where their audiences have been familiar with *God's written Narrative* from the Jewish Scriptures, it's worth noting how they engage with these people who know nothing of the true Creator. Here, understandably, they start much further back…. with a pre-evangelism appeal to the *Narrative of God's Creation* and the natural blessings of life that speak clearly of His sovereign but gracious rule over the earth. Whatever level of access people have to God's revelation, they have no excuse - everyone is morally responsible to live up to His absolute standards.

Paul recovers after being attacked

It's not long before the town's adulation turns sour (Acts 14:19,20). The orthodox Jews from Antioch and Iconium have relentlessly followed them all the way here to Lystra. Somehow they are able to turn the crowd against the two Gospel teachers. Paul is particularly targeted and is brutally pelted with stones, then dragged outside the town and left for dead. But with those from the town who have become followers of Jesus standing around, Paul regains consciousness and gets to his feet… perhaps with God's miraculous help, Luke doesn't specify. But certainly the next day he is well enough to set out with Barnabas on the hundred-kilometer trip to Derbe. Luke doesn't give many details of their time in this town that was at the very eastern edge of the Roman province of Galatia, but he does say that through their sharing of the Good News they introduce many people to Jesus Christ who become His disciples.

They revisit the churches they've planted

At this point Paul and Barnabas decide not to go on to any new communities (Acts 14:21-27). Their most direct route home would be southeast across the Taurus mountains via the narrow pass then known as the Cilician Gates… today called the Gülek Pass, route of the Tarsus-Ankara Highway in Turkey. But instead they choose to retrace their steps, visiting the towns they've been through, including those where they were so viciously harassed. They know that the fledgling churches they've planted need encouragement to stand against the many challenges they will inevitably face… and so they spend time strengthening them, no doubt teaching by building on the Narrative foundations already laid.

But the two church planters also know that these groups of disciples will need guidance and on going feeding from God's Word. No details are given here about the process, but we know that by the time Paul and Barnabas leave each fellowship they've made sure that there are qualified leaders in place. The term for this role that Luke used is *presbyterios* - traditionally translated into English as *elders*. This has links back to the Old Covenant when certain men in the Israelite tribes were looked to for guidance based on their wisdom and experience.

Now, as we'll see in the Narrative, this role of shepherding local groups of believers under the New Covenant is linked directly to particular Spirit-given gifts, abilities and personal qualities. Certainly the Acts account reflects that the two church planters took very seriously this step of appointing elders and then placing the believers into their care.

Paul and Barnabas continue to retrace their steps, until eventually they make it back to their home fellowship in Antioch of Syria. Their arrival must have been a real time of excitement and encouragement for the church that has been supporting them in prayer while they've been away. The two have great things to report…how so many Gentiles, in particular, responded in faith to the message of Good News about Jesus that they had shared with them.

? DISCUSSION POINTS

1. Explain what you understand Luke meant when he wrote "and all who were chosen for eternal life became believers" (Acts 13:48). <u>Note:</u> as you attempt to answer consider:

    a) the immediate narrative context in which the statement was made,

    b) the changes between the Old and New Covenants,

    c) what is taking place in the time of the Acts Narrative,

    d) what God has shown of Himself and His purposes throughout the entire Narrative so far.

2. Do you believe that God continues to use "miraculous signs and wonders" to validate the Gospel message today? Please explain.

3. What lessons or principles can you identify from the example of Paul and Barnabas as they revisited the believers in the cities they'd already been to? Try to describe this in terms of how you feel the Lord Jesus would want:

    a) us to relate to an individual who becomes a believer through our witness,

    b) a cross-cultural church planting team to relate to a group of new believers in a hostile community.

2.20 An important meeting and Paul revisits the new churches

OBJECTIVES OF THIS TUTORIAL

Paul and Barnabas attend a meeting in Jerusalem that considers important issues relating to the new Gentile believers. They then decide to visit the churches they'd planted on their previous trip, but they disagree over the addition of John Mark and finally go their separate ways, and Paul travels with Silas, a leader in the Jerusalem church. In southern Galatia, Paul invites a young disciple, Timothy, to join them as they go from town to town in that area strengthening the churches.
The portion of Scripture referred to in this tutorial is: Acts 15:1-16:5

Last time

When the Jews in Pisidian Antioch rejected the Gospel, Paul and Barnabas indicated that from now on they would target the Gentiles with their Message. After being evicted from that city they moved on to Iconium where they saw a church planted. Despite a campaign of slander against them, they stayed there for some time teaching God's Word. When they heard of a plot to kill them, they traveled to Lystra where they had difficulty convincing the people not to worship them as gods. After going to one more place, Derbe, they revisited the churches where they'd been, encouraging the believers and appointing elders. Eventually they arrived home in Antioch and shared about what God had done through them.

Paul and Barnabas attend an important meeting

The next part of Luke's Acts account (Acts 15:1-32) focuses on a controversy that has been simmering in the Church almost from the beginning. At its most fundamental level, the dispute is about how a person can be declared righteous by God. As we've seen, among those who identify with the Church there are some who acknowledge Jesus as the Messiah, but who also insist that the Law given to Moses must be followed, New Covenant or not. Some of them come down to Antioch of Syria and begin teaching dogmatically that a man who is not circumcised cannot be saved… faith in Jesus Christ is not enough. Understandably, after what they've just experienced on their recent church planting trip among the Gentiles, Paul and Barnabas disagree strongly with them.

The Antioch church decides that it needs help to resolve this issue. Paul and Barnabas along with others are sent to Jerusalem to discuss it with the Apostles and elders. There's no sense in the Acts Narrative of a denominational hierarchy being created, but we do see a healthy interdependence. And in this case we see a local church reaching out to seek counsel from other godly leaders, and humbly submitting to the authority of the Lord's Apostles.

After extensive discussions in Jerusalem, Peter declares his position, which is that clearly God has accepted Gentiles based solely on their faith, and has confirmed this by giving them the Holy Spirit. Why then, he asks, should they be burdened with Jewish laws and traditions, which no one can ever perfectly fulfill anyway? He sums up with this profound statement, "We believe that we are all saved the same way, by the undeserved grace of the Lord Jesus." Then Paul and Barnabas are given opportunity to share the amazing and indisputable evidence of God's blessing that they experienced during their recent trip into the predominantly Gentile communities.

Finally, James, one of the other key leaders in the Jerusalem church, takes the floor. He quotes the prophet Amos to show that Gentile people coming to faith apart from the Law is something God always intended. Then he summarizes the decisions of this meeting that has become known as *the Jerusalem Council*... Guided by God's Spirit they feel there should be no obligation on Gentile believers to follow the Jewish Law... but they should keep clear of the idolatry and immorality of their former cultish associations, and also avoid eating meat with blood - something that would be very offensive to their Jewish brothers and sisters. A letter spelling out these conclusions is given to Paul, Barnabas and two leaders chosen by the Jerusalem church, Judas and Silas. When they get back and read it out in the Antioch church it comes as a real encouragement to the believers, many of whom as we know, are Gentiles.

Paul and Barnabas head off on separate teams

Some time passes during which Paul and Barnabas continue to work in Antioch, sharing God's Word (Acts 15:36-41). When Paul suggests a return visit to the churches they'd planted on their previous trip, Barnabas is enthusiastic. This highlights again the concern the two church planters obviously have for those who've come to faith through their testimony. Later Paul will use many metaphors to describe this sense of responsibility he feels for the churches he has planted, perhaps the most striking being that of a mother with a newborn baby.

Even though they fully concur on the need for a follow-up visit to the churches, they have very different opinions on the issue of team members. Paul strongly disagrees with Barnabas' idea of inviting John Mark again... No way, he deserted before in Pamphylia. How can you trust someone like that again? Feelings are so strong they decide to go their separate ways. The Spirit doesn't lead Luke to comment on the rights and wrongs of this situation, so we have to be careful in imposing our own conclusions. Perhaps we are to understand that the Holy Spirit was guiding both in their respective viewpoints, and that having two teams head out at this point is what He intends.

So Barnabas takes his cousin, John Mark, and leaves for his home island of Cyprus, while Paul invites Silas to travel with him as he heads north then west through the regions of Syria and Cilicia. Silas - also known by his Latin name Silvanus - is a good choice for Paul's church strengthening and planting team. He is a well-regarded leader from the Jerusalem fellowship and gifted by the Spirit as a prophet. The church at Antioch knows him from his recent visit, and they are able to confidently send him out with Paul on this new initiative. Also, as the Narrative will soon note, like Paul, he enjoys the legal protection of being a Roman citizen.

A young man, Timothy, joins Paul's team

The first place they visit, on what has become know as *Paul's Second Missionary Journey*, is Derbe... then on to Lystra, the place where Paul nearly died last time after an angry crowd tried to kill him with stones. Here (Acts 16:1-5) we meet for the first time a young man of mixed Greek and Jewish descent who will play a significant role in the Acts Narrative and the early expansion of the Church: Timothy. We don't know if Timothy first accepts the Gospel through Paul's teaching or through the testimony of his mother and grandmother, also committed followers of Jesus. Luke notes that he is "well thought of by the believers in Lystra and Iconium": in other words, the churches in that part of Galatia. It's worth remembering that only a few short years before, none of these fellowships existed. Now, because Paul and Barnabas were willing to take the Good News to those communities, there are groups - local *ecclesia* - of God's children there who are able to share God's life-giving Narrative with others.

Luke calls Timothy a *disciple* - just one of the ways the Narrative refers to those who've believed in Jesus for salvation. The Greek word he uses is *mathétés*, referring to someone who follows the instructions of an individual and/or a body of teaching. Later this would be translated into Latin as *discipulus*, and then into English as *disciple*. Earlier, in the account of their initial visit to this area, the text says that Paul and Barnabas were "preaching the Good News... and making disciples" (Acts 14:21). This, of course, is exactly what Jesus had authorized His Apostles - and through them His entire *Ecclesia* - to do. It also connects with an important Narrative thread we've been following... how from the beginning God has been delegating real responsibility to His image-bearers who humbly walk with Him. It's something that flows from God's character and forms an important part of His overall purposes. Now Paul, who's been helped himself by others on this road of following Jesus, commits to doing the same with Timothy. He invites the young disciple to join their team and in time, as we'll see, Paul will entrust Timothy with major discipleship responsibilities himself.

There's an instructive side note to Timothy's inclusion. Having grown up in his father's house that's dominated by Greek rather than Jewish cultural norms, Timothy has not been circumcised. It's interesting that Paul, who is so quick to resist any mingling of Jewish rules and traditions with the Good News, arranges for Timothy to be circumcised before he joins the team. Clearly this has nothing to do with his standing in God's eyes... instead, Paul's intention is that as God's workmen they should avoid anything that will get in the way of people hearing truth. He very firmly believes that representatives of the Lord Jesus should become whatever they need to be, so that if people walk away it's because they're rejecting the Good News, not because they've been personally or culturally offended.

The team, led by Paul and Silas, moves on from Lystra, visiting the local *ecclesia* - gatherings of disciples - in the different towns. Their visits strengthen the believers in their faith and more people are saved and added to the churches. As we've already noted, and as we'll continue to see in the Acts account and beyond, Paul assumes a very real sense of responsibility for the individuals and groups of God's children who've come to faith through his sharing of the Good News. He is aware that there is a long way to go for them to 'grow up', as it were, in the faith... and for that to happen they will need to be taught God's Word and discipled in a way that helps them move from spiritual infanthood to maturity.

 **DISCUSSION POINTS**

1. Describe some of the dynamics that you think made this issue of the Jewish Law, and particularly circumcision, such a tenacious problem for the early Church. Given that our historic and cultural situation is obviously very different, do you feel there are any related areas of confusion that churches in our society could struggle with?

2. Despite taking opposite stances, do you think it is possible that both Paul and Barnabas were correct in their respective decisions about whether or not to invite John Mark along again? Please explain your answer.

3. What has been your experience in regard to discipleship? Has anyone more experienced in the faith played a significant role of helping you along consistently? Have you ever played that role with anyone else? How would you describe: (1) the goal(s) of this kind of relationship, (2) the key elements that make it effective?

4. While circumcision is unlikely to be an issue now, give some examples of the personal and cultural adjustments that you feel you could make to be a more effective witness for the Lord in your current context with people you already know. Then briefly do the same for (1) another sub-culture in this country, (2) a different country and culture you know something about. <u>Note:</u> Try to picture the whole range of things that you might need to change or be willing to give up - tangible and otherwise.

2.21 The Holy Spirit guides Paul & his companions to Philippi

✓ OBJECTIVES OF THIS TUTORIAL

After visiting the existing fellowships in southern Galatia, Paul and his church planting team are keen to visit communities that don't yet have access to the Gospel. With the Holy Spirit's guidance, they travel to the city of Philippi.
The portion of Scripture referred to in this tutorial is: **Acts 16:6-40**

Last time

Paul and Barnabas attended a meeting, or 'Council' in Jerusalem that considered the issue of whether Gentiles needed to be circumcised and follow the Jewish religious laws. They gratefully returned to Antioch with the decision of the Apostles and church leaders who agreed that it was unnecessary because salvation is the result of God's grace, not human effort.

Paul and Barnabas decided to visit the churches they'd planted on their previous trip, but they disagreed over the addition of John Mark and finally went their separate ways. Paul invited Silas, a leader in the Jerusalem church, to travel with him. In southern Galatia, he invited a young disciple, Timothy, to join them, and the team went from town to town in that area strengthening the churches.

With God's guidance the team heads to Macedonia

But now Paul is keen to take the Gospel to new areas. He plans to travel southwest into the Roman province of Asia. However, the account says the Holy Spirit stops this from happening. We're not told how the Spirit makes it clear that they should not head that direction, or why. What we can take from this though, is that there's nothing wrong with having plans laid out, but we need to be open to God's guidance in the actual implementation. This is how it is meant to work in the very real partnership that God delights in having with His people.

Heading across the region called Mysia, they eventually reach Troas, a port on the Aegean Sea, near the northern tip of Turkey's western coast (Acts 16:6-10). With the

Spirit having made it clear for a second time that plans they've laid out don't line up with His, Paul and his companions may have been feeling some confusion about what to do next. But because they are looking to God for guidance, He does indeed find a way to direct them. During the night, the Spirit shows Paul a compelling vision... a man is there pleading with him "Come over to Macedonia and help us!" In a way this man, whether a real individual or not, represents for us all the people in our time who desperately need someone to come and help them... to give them access to the Words of Life. God will faithfully guide us to opportunities to help where it is most needed if we honestly make ourselves available to Him.

The team doesn't hang around debating how they should respond: the text says that they leave *at once* for Macedonia...the Greek homeland of Alexander the Great and now a province of Rome. They find a ship that's about to leave on the 200 kilometer voyage northwest across the Aegean and, after overnighting on the mountainous island of Samothrace to avoid the dangers of night sailing, they land in Neapolis the following day. Walking along the well-made Roman road - the Via Egnatia, or Egnatian Way, parts of which can be still seen today - it would have taken them 2 or 3 hours to reach Philippi. Luke, who by now is writing this account in the first person "we", apparently having joined Paul's team in Troas, describes Philippi as "a major city of that district of Macedonia and a Roman colony." There are quite a few Biblical scholars who feel that Luke was actually a doctor from this city, although others feel there is more evidence for Antioch in Syria being his home town.

The church in Philippi starts as Lydia is saved

The beginnings of the church in Philippi, that would one day become so well known in the ongoing Narrative, are anything but dramatic (Acts 16:2-15). Paul and the others have had a few days in the city, perhaps being shown around by Luke so they can get a feel for this cosmopolitan city that is proud of its standing in the Roman Empire. But now it's Saturday, the Sabbath. There's no significant Jewish community and therefore no synagogue, but it's not hard to find the handful of people around here who worship our One True God. Yes, just as you'd expect, they've gathered down by the river to pray... mostly women today.

It's pleasant sitting here with the water rippling past, away from the hustle and bustle of the city, sharing the Gospel with people who are interested. Particularly one lady who says her name is Lydia. She's actually from Thyatira, way over there in Asia Minor, probably an agent or buyer for a manufacturer of the famous purple cloth they make there. Possibly she attended the synagogue there before moving here to Philippi. Whatever her history, the Lord has obviously prepared her heart because as she sits listening to Paul sharing the truth there's no doubt that she's wholeheartedly accepting the Good News about Jesus.

Before long, others from Lydia's family and no doubt people working for them, have also put their faith in Jesus Christ, and they are all baptized. The Narrative doesn't spell it out, but it seems fairly certain that it's in this home that the Philippi church, that we'll hear so much more about, has its start. It's worth noting that this really represents a much more common scenario for the expansion of the *Ecclesia* than the spectacular, headline events like Pentecost. We've seen some instances in Acts of barriers being dramatically breached by the Gospel in a great rush, with miraculous signs and large numbers of people being added, but these events are in the minority. Most often, in the time of the Apostles and since, it has been a quiet but steady trickle moving out in many directions at once… through God's children being willing to put themselves in situations where they are ready and able to share truth clearly with whoever is willing to listen.

Many times, like here in Philippi, local fellowships begin with one opportunity being taken to share with a heart that is ready; with a commitment being made to share God's Narrative with one family or group of friends; when the patience and effort needed to build genuine relationships bears fruit; when new believers through their lives and testimony begin to draw others. A church is formed when the Lord gradually brings those people together to make a 'body', gathering them around the teaching of His Word, helping them respond together in genuine worship, equipping them to function and be a light in that context, giving them a common identity and sense of purpose. Of course God's Spirit can and does sometimes use events to create dynamics, which prepare a number of people - even an entire community - to come to faith at the same time. These sudden forward surges of the Gospel are important landmarks in the Task that we can certainly celebrate… but we should be just as quick to see God's purposes being accomplished when an individual like Lydia comes to faith and, in time, becomes an integral part of a local fellowship.

Paul and Silas are wrongly beaten and jailed

The peaceful start to their time in Philippi doesn't last (Acts 16:16-25). Being part of a church planting team with Paul is rarely boring. When he, in the name of Jesus Christ, commands demons to leave a slave-girl who they've been controlling, her owners are outraged. It's not completely clear from the text whether the evil spirits actually had a genuine ability to see the future or not, but this girl certainly has a reputation in the area as a fortune-teller. No doubt it has been her abnormal behavior and the strange voices coming from her mouth that convinced people she was receiving prophetic powers from the "python spirit" of Greek mythology.

Whatever the case, realizing their money source has suddenly dried up, the men who've been exploiting the girl turn their anger on Paul and Silas. They drag them before the authorities and loudly accuse the two church planters of being Jews who are teaching customs that are illegal for them as Romans. Many residents of Philippi, like Paul's home town of Tarsus and other cities in the Empire, had been granted Roman citizenship in the past. Accusing them as Jews is likely to play on prejudices, because quite recently all Jews - as Luke mentions soon in the Narrative (Acts 18:2) - have been expelled from Rome... possibly because of the Christian teaching that is gaining momentum in the Empire's capital and causing concern for the Emperor. The Philippi officials listen to popular opinion - the two visitors are beaten with rods, and then locked up without real trial in the town prison.

So there they are...no doubt it's a dark, windowless, filthy cell where they are sitting with their feet clamped in heavy wooden stocks, unable to turn or change position. So what has gone wrong? Did they make a mistake when they thought God's Spirit was guiding them here to Macedonia, instead of Asia? How are they supposed to do anything worthwhile now? Is this what they get for giving up the comforts, security and fellowship back home?! Don't the Lord's servants have any rights? But no, their co-worker Luke records a very different picture of the two men. Of course we don't know everything they are feeling, but his description of them praying together and singing hymns of praise loudly enough for the other prisoners to hear certainly reflects contentment and even gratitude for the circumstances they find themselves in.

After an earthquake the jailer comes to faith

The story of what happens next is familiar (Acts 16:26-34). The jailer, asleep. What is that? What's going on? A nightmare? No, it's real. Everything's moving, swaying, crashing. He's standing now, barely awake, every door in the jail wide open. The prisoners must be gone, every one! I'll pay for this, with my life. There will be no mercy. Better to just finish it...a quick thrust with a sword in my throat. But wait, who's that calling out? A voice from the darkness, "Stop! Don't kill yourself! We're all here!" Oh, the relief. It's those Jews, who've been teaching about how God sent His own Son... to be a sacrifice. "Hey, someone bring a light. Come out, come out. Please, tell me how I can be saved. Oh, so it's nothing I have to *do*, nothing I *can* do, just believe in Him, in the Lord Jesus... He did it all! Yes, I believe that. I believe in Him. Now, let's get your wounds cleaned, and get you something to eat. I want you to share all of this with my family."

They get an official apology before leaving town

The next morning the city officials have changed their attitudes. Something has alerted them that they have acted inappropriately (Acts 16:35-40). But Paul is not going to go quietly. As Roman citizens their rights have been violated. He wants a public apology... perhaps he's thinking about the young Philippi church and wants the authorities on the back foot so the believers will be left in peace. Paul knows that they receive their ultimate authority to undertake their church planting objectives from the One who'd sent them out in the first place, the One who said He'd always be with them. The world system and those who pursue power within it are never going to be sympathetic to the true mission of the Church. But clearly Paul also knows that when God chooses to, He can use human authorities and laws to provide a context in which His truth can spread and His Body can prosper. In the Narrative so far, we've seen examples of God using both official persecution and protection to further His objective. As His co-workers we need to be alert to the opportunities He brings along and ask for the grace and wisdom, the courage and contentment, to participate in what He is doing at any given time.

Luke concludes the story of this time in Philippi with the comment that before leaving town, Paul and Silas go to the home of Lydia to meet with the believers and encourage them again. For the next section of the Narrative, Luke resumes telling the story of the church planting team's adventures in the second person: "they". He will join them again later, but it's thought by some that he's staying in Philippi for now, to help establish and strengthen the new *ecclesia* there.

THE HOLY SPIRIT GUIDES PAUL & HIS COMPANIONS TO PHILIPPI

? DISCUSSION POINTS

1. What are some things that stand out to you from the Acts account about how the believers received guidance from God? Do you think that we can be led by God in the same way today, or are there some differences? Do you find the process of discerning God's will challenging, or are you generally confident that you know what He wants you to do?

2. Can you easily see yourself walking up to the people by the river in Philippi that morning and getting into a conversation that results in you sharing the Gospel... or is that hard to imagine? If you were there and had begun to talk with Lydia, how would you go about it? What guiding principles, if any, do you think would be good to have in mind?

3. In light of the whole Narrative, do you think that we, as believers, have any 'rights'? What about those sent out to be involved in new church planting initiatives? Can God's children and workers expect some level of protection? Please explain.

2.22 Paul continues visiting & teaching in the Aegean area

OBJECTIVES OF THIS TUTORIAL

Paul and his team travel to Thessalonica, then Paul and Silas move on to Berea. When opponents of the truth make further work impossible, Paul goes to Athens, where he gives his famous speech to the intellectuals of the city on Mars Hill. He then travels to Corinth where he stays for around two years teaching God's Word, before heading back to Antioch via Ephesus and Jerusalem.

The portion of Scripture referred to in this tutorial is: **Acts 17:1-18:22**

Last time

After visiting the existing fellowships in southern Galatia, Paul and his church planting team were keen to visit communities that didn't yet have access to the Gospel. With the Holy Spirit's guidance, they traveled to the city of Philippi in the province of Macedonia. There a woman, Lydia, was saved along with her family, and their home became the base for the Philippian church. Paul and Silas were beaten and jailed. Their jailer, waking in the night to find an earthquake had opened all the doors, was about to kill himself. Paul stopped him, explaining that everyone was still there. The relieved man accepted the Gospel message and he and his family were saved. After encouraging the new believers again, Paul's team left Philippi.

The team visits Thessalonica

Heading out again, Paul, Silas, young Timothy, and any others with them, would have been following the *Via Egnatia*... an epic Roman road that stretches way back to the east behind them to Byzantium on the Black Sea - today's Istanbul - and ahead all the way to the Adriatic coast in modern day Albania. They pass through a couple of towns, apparently without staying long, until they reach Thessalonica, about 160 kilometers west of Philippi (Acts 17:1-10). Thessalonica had an estimated population of 200,000 when Paul visited - at the time it was the largest city in Macedonia - and today is the second largest in all of Greece.

Typically, Paul visits the synagogue, knowing that he has an immediate point of contact with people who are familiar with the true God from the Jewish Scriptures. He draws out the truth for them, particularly from those sections that clearly point forward to Jesus as the promised Messiah. Here as always, we see Paul carefully sharing truth by laying worldview, Narrative foundations or building on whatever he finds already in place. Having taken the time to do this, he's then able to present the incarnation, death and resurrection of Jesus as the logical climax of all that God has been working towards down through history. So then it's not some optional religious system he's offering; instead it can be seen as the only possible solution a Creator who's completely holy and completely loving would come to, as He seeks to rescue His lost race of image-bearers.

This clear message resonates with many… Luke says they are *persuaded*. A couple of years later, in one of the letters Paul will write to them as a local fellowship, he'll remind them that they were saved through God's Spirit and through their belief in the truth (2 Thessalonians 2:13). Their new birth comes as they willingly accept what the Spirit reveals to them miraculously in their hearts or *spirits*, while also convincing them logically through their minds, or *reason*. Some of those who are saved are Jews, but many more are men and women from the majority Greek or Roman culture who've been associated with the synagogue.

The now familiar pattern for Paul's visits to different places repeats itself…the orthodox Jews are upset at losing influence over these former adherents to their faith, some of whom are prominent people in the community. Accusations are made, a mob gathers, a riot starts…"It's those troublemakers from Judea. What are their names, Paul and Silas? We've heard about them. Going around teaching about this Jesus… saying he's the real king. Causing disturbances everywhere. Well not here. The Romans will call it treason! We'll lose our status as a free city. They're at the house of that Jew, Jason. Right, let's get them." Not finding Paul and Silas, they take Jason and others to the city council, but they are eventually released after posting a good behavior bond.

The new believers feel that under the circumstances it's best for Paul and Silas to move on that same night. Luke mentions Paul speaking at the synagogue in Thessalonica on three consecutive weeks, but it's not entirely clear if that's the full extent of their stay in the city. However long it is, by the time Paul and the team leave, there is a group of believers in the city with a deep commitment to the Lord Jesus, a common sense of identity, a good grasp of the fundamental truths of the faith, and an understanding of their role in the community. As Paul will write in a letter to them soon, they have the strength to stand against the opposition, which inevitably came. That said, there are some important areas of truth that he did not have time to share with them before his hasty departure, and those are some of the topics he'll address soon in the two letters to the Thessalonian church that we have recorded in the New Testament.

In Berea they find people keen to engage

Continuing west on the *Via Egnatia* for 70 kilometers they reach Berea - today Veria - at the eastern foot of the Vermio Mountains (Acts 17:10-15). They find people in the synagogue here who are open to the truth they are proclaiming and who listen eagerly, as the text says, to Paul's message. But their enthusiasm for the teaching of the church planters is not mindless acceptance. Day after day, Luke says, they search the Scriptures - God's Narrative - to verify that what Paul and Silas are teaching aligns with what God Himself has revealed there. And, as a direct result of them truly grasping these things for themselves, many from both the Jewish minority and Greek majority believe in the Good News about Jesus.

As we've noted before, God created us *in His image* so that we can respond to His revelation of Himself fully: with our hearts, souls, emotions, wills and minds. When we tell God's Story to people, we need skill and insight so that they are hearing *Him* appealing to the deepest longings of their hearts, captivating their imaginations, challenging their worldview assumptions, and convincing them of the inherent logic and coherence in everything He has said and done.

Almost inevitably it seems, Jews from Thessalonica follow the church planters to Berea and stir up problems. The new believers act quickly and escort Paul to Athens... probably by sea, although Luke doesn't say specifically. Silas and Timothy stay behind for a while before rejoining Paul, no doubt to strengthen the young church.

Paul visits Athens and speaks on Mars Hill

Meanwhile Paul isn't relaxing while he's waiting for them in Athens. Home to an estimated 20,000 people, at the time of his visit, it's well past its prime of five centuries before when it dominated the other Greek city states and was renowned as a center of Hellenist literature, art and philosophy. At the time of Paul's visit there is still plenty of outstanding architecture to see, and as he looks around, something else is impossible to miss (Acts 17:16-32). The first century Greek historian, Plutarch, recorded that there were 20,000 statues of gods in Athens, and the Roman writer Petronius from around that time famously joked that it was easier to find a god in Athens than a man. It's not surprising to hear that Paul is really bothered at this visible evidence of paganism everywhere he goes. How do you begin to create a hunger for the Gospel in a society that has turned so far from the true God?

His approach to the situation is worth noting... he tries to pursue meaningful engagement with people in two different contexts. The first is a religious setting - the *synagogue* - where there is already a foundation of understanding about the true God to build on. The second context is out in the *public arena* where almost no one he interacts with knows anything about God or His Narrative. The more educated of this group tend to have a worldview that syncretizes their extreme polytheism with the teachings of two respective schools of philosophy. The Epicureans pursue meaning through restraint, tranquility, enjoying life, loving others and avoiding any fear of death. The other, the Stoics, are looking for fulfillment through conforming their wills to an impersonal god-force: 'reason', that they believe rules the universe.

At first Paul's teaching is seen by these intellectuals as bizarre and foreign, but the longer they debate with him, the more intrigued they become. They invite him to address the Council that gives oversight to religion and education for the city. Most believe this meeting takes place on Mars Hill, just below the famous fortified *acropolis*. Paul's speech provides us with an invaluable example of how to engage with people who have no prior knowledge of the true Creator-God. He looks for common ground, and begins with something familiar: their altar "to an Unknown God", but he reinterprets it in an unexpected way to get their attention. Then he introduces them to God, briefly describing His being, His character, His purpose for creation and stance towards sinful human beings… introducing the truth that this God is infinitely greater than any of their false deities. Embedded in his address are a number of significant challenges to their existing worldview. He concludes with a warning and an exhortation for them to seek understanding about what God has provided for humans to be able to be reunited with Him. Time doesn't permit us to analyze Paul's famous sermon in depth, but anyone will be rewarded by a careful study of it in order to glean underlying principles for sharing truth. Some of his audience responds with contempt, but others, including one member of the Council, become believers as a result.

Paul travels to Corinth for a lengthy stay

Without giving any particular reason, Luke records that Paul decides to leave Athens and head to Corinth (Acts 18:1-22)…maybe in the hope of finding more prepared soil for the Gospel message. Today just an hour and a half by train or road, Paul would probably have walked the 80 kilometers around the coast. It seems that as he approached the big bustling city of around 200,000 people, it probably wasn't with a spring in his step. He'd later write to the church he'd plant there that as he came, he was very conscious of his own weakness…in fact, he describes himself as timid and trembling (1 Corinthians 2:3). We don't know for sure all the factors playing into his state of mind, but for one thing, he was on his own - Silas and Timothy hadn't caught up with him yet. We also learn later that he was in a tough spot financially. And Corinth itself was a daunting prospect. Much of its population was made up of sailors, merchants, refugees, and discharged soldiers. The cultic prostitution at the temple of Aphrodite had brought wealth but also corruption to Corinthian society, and its name was synonymous with immorality.

But the Lord Jesus is looking after the former Pharisee He'd called into His service so dramatically on the road to Damascus. Just as He'd promised nearly a quarter of a century before, wherever His disciples go out to share His Good News, He is with them, giving them strength and guidance. In Corinth, Paul meets a Jewish couple who've recently come there from Rome after the Emperor banished all Jews from the capital city. He is able to live and work with them at their mutual trade of tent making. We don't know at what point this couple become believers - whether previously, or through Paul's witness - but later in the Narrative we'll hear that they play an important role as co-workers with him in his church planting and establishing work. So during the week he works at his trade and then on Saturdays - the Sabbath - he regularly goes to the local synagogue to look for opportunities to share the Gospel with Jews and people from other ethnicities who worship the One, True, God there.

Eventually, after Timothy and Silas arrive with a gift of money from the believers in Philippi, he's able to spend all his time sharing God's Word with people. It's worth nothing that while there's nothing wrong with the categories of supporter, full-time worker, supported missionary, or tent maker that we use today, they don't seem to apply to Paul or his co-workers. For him there is no dichotomy, no distinction. Being a witness for his Master, being a church planter, these are not roles he takes on or puts off at certain times... it is just who he is. He's simply living out in any given situation what he understands he has been given to do, and what he's responsible for, as someone who's benefited so much from God's grace.

After most of the Jews in Corinth take a stance of opposition to Paul and the Gospel, he says that he is no longer responsible for them... he'll now focus on taking the truth to the other ethnic groups. He finds a great base to work from and some more co-workers in the city. Although Luke records that Paul's efforts result in a lot of people coming to faith, it seems that at some point Paul becomes disheartened or intimidated. The Lord encourages him not to be afraid, not to stop sharing... and reminds His servant that He is with him. Once again we're reminded of God's amazing intention to work alongside those who'll faithfully walk with Him. He has given Paul the role of being His Narrator, His Voice, but the final results are His responsibility. It's His church that is being built, His people that are being equipped. This strengthens Paul's resolve and he stays there in Corinth this time for a year and a half teaching God's Word. It was during this time in Corinth that Paul wrote the two letters to the Thessalonians that are preserved in the New Testament. Paul now heads home, taking Priscilla and Aquila with him as far as Ephesus. It seems that Timothy and Silas stayed in Macedonia and Achaia province, probably to continue giving guidance to the new churches there. On the voyage back to Palestine, Paul stops off briefly in Ephesus. When the Jews there invite him to stay longer, he promises to come back again if God works it out that way. The ship lands in Caesarea and he visits the church in Jerusalem before finally making it back to his sending church in Antioch of Syria.

? DISCUSSION POINTS

1. What are you understanding from the Narrative is our role in persuading people about the truth? What is the Holy Spirit's role? Can you draw out any general principles from the Acts account about how we can play our part? (Note: We're focusing here on how people become convinced in their *minds*, but there are, of course, other dimensions such as *emotion* and *will* involved in the process of coming to faith.)

2. Picture yourself being involved in a church planting effort in a community where there are no other believers... what do you expect would be the most likely sources of discouragement for you personally? How do you think you'd try to deal with that? What principles embedded in the Acts Narrative would be good to remember if you were struggling with discouragement?

3. How much financial security do you feel that we can expect as God's children and co-workers? Should there be a different level of expectation for those who stay in their home churches and those who move to a different community as church planters? What responsibility do parents (in the latter situation) have to ensure their children have all the same opportunities as kids who grow up in their home society?

➡ ACTIVITIES

1. Do some research on the contemporary movement of 'tent-making' in missions. Then in less than a page explain why you feel: (1) Proponents of this approach do or do not have adequate support from the Acts account for their claims, (2) The approach is always, never, or sometimes, a good idea in light of the Great Commission and current realities.

 Paul teaches in Ephesus, with widespread results

 OBJECTIVES OF THIS TUTORIAL

After a time in Syrian Antioch, Paul sets out on his third major church planting and establishing trip. After traveling across country he eventually arrives in Ephesus. Paul stays in Ephesus for at least two more years, teaching the truth with widespread results throughout the entire region.

The portion of Scripture referred to in this tutorial is: Acts 18:23-19:10

Last time

Paul and his team traveled to Thessalonica where a number of people were persuaded by the Gospel message and a church was planted. When trouble began to brew, Paul and Silas moved on to Berea. Here their audience is noted for the care they took in studying God's Word for themselves to verify that the visitors' teaching was accurate. When opponents of the truth made further work impossible, Paul went to Athens, where he gave his famous speech to the intellectuals of the city on Mars Hill. He then traveled to Corinth where he found accommodation and work with a couple, Priscilla and Aquila. Paul stayed in Corinth for around two years teaching God's Word, before concluding what is known as his *second missionary journey* by heading back to Antioch via Ephesus and Jerusalem.

Paul starts his third church planting trip

Paul probably stays in Antioch of Syria for as much as six months before heading off again to visit the churches in the region of Asia Minor... the area we know today as Anatolia in Turkey (Acts 18:23). He is not planting new churches but rather strengthening those already there. It's clear that Paul does not take on himself the responsibility of sharing the Gospel with every person or even every community. Having seen a group saved, he *does* take on a long-term role of continuing to strengthen, challenge, equip and even correct when they are moving away from the truth. But from the letters we have recorded that he's writing to these groups of believers, it's clear that he wants to see *them* reaching out to their own communities and beyond, as a natural outcome of their growing maturity in Christ.

It should also be noted that as he visits these churches, he's not functioning as their overall leader or *bishop*, in a hierarchical sense. He and his co-workers have not created a denomination. The Lord has given him the status of *Apostle*, with all the inherent authority in being one of God's human spokesmen during this period when the written Narrative is being completed. And so there are times where he does speak to the churches from the platform of *Apostolic authority*... but even then it is something he uses sparingly and carefully. Paul understands that his role is to equip individuals and teams of leaders within the local *ecclesia* to function *under* and *through* the authority of God's revealed Word so *they* can encourage, guide, equip and correct the believers entrusted to their care.

A promising new teacher comes to Ephesus

Luke inserts a "meanwhile" here as he takes a moment to explain what has been happening in Ephesus, which is where Paul will spend a large chunk of his time on what has become known as his *third missionary journey (Acts 18:24-28)*. We'll remember that on his voyage back to Syria at the end of his last expedition, Paul stopped briefly in this city that was the capital of the province of Asia. Finding interest in the Gospel message in the synagogue, he'd promised that he would come back.

In the meantime, while he's been in Antioch and now traveling across country visiting the churches, Paul's friends Priscilla and Aquila have been busy. They've come to know a Jewish man, Apollos, who has moved to Ephesus from his home city of Alexandria, 800 kilometers across the Mediterranean in Egypt. Somehow he has heard of and believed in Jesus the Messiah, even passionately preaching about Him in the synagogue, but there are some fundamentals he's not clear about. For example, he doesn't understand the meaning of baptism under the New Covenant or about the Holy Spirit's role. But Paul's tent-making friends, Priscilla and Aquila, have been faithfully helping Apollos understand more of the Narrative, and their efforts bear fruit...he will go on to be a very effective teacher of God's Word among the churches in the area. In fact, while Paul is headed towards Ephesus from the east, Apollos is visiting the believers in Corinth where he proves to be a powerful apologist for the Gospel message.

God gives powerful evidence of the Spirit's presence

So Paul finally reaches the Aegean coast, having come across country from Antioch in Syria, a journey of around 1000 kilometers (Acts 19:1-6). What he sees as he arrives is an impressive city spread over two hills with the Cayster River mouth between, forming an excellent harbor... although in the centuries ahead, this will silt up, eventually causing the city to be abandoned. Ephesus is probably the fourth largest city in the world at this time, home to quarter of a million people. This city, where he'll end up living and working for the next three years, is widely renowned for its architecturally magnificent temple to the goddess *Artemis*.

He is immediately immersed in the things his life has been all about for many years now, sharing the truth about the Lord Jesus Christ. He finds that there are a handful of people in Ephesus who've already come to believe in Jesus as Messiah, probably as the result of the witness of Apollos. Naturally enough, given the gaps in their teacher's understanding, they are missing some areas of truth. The only type of baptism they know about is what John had done in the Jordan river for people who wanted to repent and prepare their hearts for the coming Messiah. But now, when Paul explains, these followers of Christ are glad to go through the simple baptism ceremony for the New Covenant. They also hear from Paul for the first time how, under the New Covenant, God's Spirit comes to live permanently in people when they come to faith. So now, to reinforce this reality, God chooses to show the Spirit's presence with them in a kind of mini-Pentecost. Paul puts his hand on their heads and no doubt asks God to give these young believers and others around a special demonstration of how the Spirit fills His people and equips them as His witnesses. God graciously does exactly that, and they are suddenly able to speak in other languages and communicate truth directly from God - to *prophesy*.

Events like these, during this period when God is allowing people to see tangible evidence of the Holy Spirit's full presence with them, must have been incredibly exciting. But it's important for us to clearly understand the full extent of what God has revealed to us in our time through His written Narrative. If we do have the correct perspective and value the most important things, we are able to recognize the exciting evidence of His presence with us and His powerful work in the world today, even if it looks different from the dramatic signs He gave at certain key points in the transitional time of the Apostles. And if we have opportunity, like Paul did in Ephesus, we can share His Narrative with others in such a way that they glimpse the amazing possibilities now open to them as the permanent, earthly residence and co-workers of the all-powerful Spirit Creator.

Paul and the believers leave the synagogue

Paul spends the next three months in Ephesus, as he'd promised on his previous stay, concentrating on sharing in the synagogue setting where people are familiar with the Old Testament Narrative. No doubt using that as a starting point, he is able to show very clearly how it has been God's plan all along for Jesus to break the power of Satan, the usurper, and lay the foundations for ultimately bringing all of creation back under God's sovereign rule. But even though his message is clear, some of those he's been interacting with choose to reject the truth, even publicly voicing their opposition to Jesus' claims of being the only Way to God (Acts 19:8-9).

Luke records that in the face of this rejection, Paul stops sharing truth in the synagogue. And, even more significantly, he encourages those who have believed to break from their association there and develop a separate identity. Paul's decision to guide the believers in this way is worth noting. Without making the mistake of developing dogma from one incident, we can simply observe that in this instance, the Apostle can see that remaining *inside* the existing religious structure will not be the best thing - either for those who've rejected the truth that has so clearly been shared with them, or for the young believers.

We should also remember that this is probably not just a casual matter of no longer turning up at the synagogue for Sabbath meetings. For some of them at least, this must surely involve rejection by their families and community and being accused of turning away from their religious and social heritage in favor of this "new Jesus cult". We don't know if some perhaps argued that they'd have more chance of reaching their Jewish community by staying *inside* the synagogue setting… all we can say is that from his experience and God-given wisdom, Paul encourages them to make a clean break as a group of believers. They will go on to become the church to whom he'll write the letter that is preserved in the New Testament.

Paul's teaching has widespread impact

Over the next couple of years, Paul teaches regularly in a lecture hall in Ephesus, and whether through his own work or through existing co-workers or new believers that he equips, the Gospel spreads throughout the province of Asia (Acts 19:9,10). It seems likely that it is during this time that three churches are established in a cluster of communities - Laodicea, Hierapolis and Colossae - at the foot of Mount Cadmus, around 160 kilometers to the east of Ephesus. In a letter Paul will later write to the Colossian believers, he mentions that even though he cares deeply for them and the other churches in the area, he has never met them in person, e.g: (Colossians 1:4-9, 2:1). So whether as a result of Paul's teaching and discipleship in Ephesus during this time, or through people who were saved on his previous travels to the north, churches are being planted as an outcome of Paul's teaching and discipleship but without his direct involvement.

When we think of Paul involved in his ministry, we often focus on the opposition he faces, the beatings, the imprisonment and so on. But something else worth noting and drawing inspiration from is his diligence and hard work. At times it is physical discipline, getting up and on the road each day until evening, to cover the thousands of kilometers he travels as he visits different places. There are also the times when he's working at his trade to pay his own way and not be a burden on the local believers. Another kind of hard work is involved in constantly meeting and talking with people, building friendships, listening to them, and looking for ways to move the conversation on to the deeper things. And then there is the task of teaching truth, day after day. Of course that is challenging when it's in the face of indifference and hostility; but even when it is with a group of hungry young believers, the burden of encouraging, guiding and helping them to apply truth for months on end involves a great deal of commitment and perseverance on Paul's part. During this time and later in prison, Paul will conscientiously be writing down truth revealed to him by the Spirit that he'll send in letters to individuals and to churches. Putting in the effort to think and write for hours is yet another kind of discipline that perhaps he didn't naturally relish. And finally - something we don't often think of as hard work - he will later describe in those letters how he is in prayer for specific people and local groups, actively, and even rigorously, entrusting them into the Lord's care.

PAUL TEACHES IN EPHESUS, WITH WIDESPREAD RESULTS

? DISCUSSION POINTS

1. Is there anything you can see in God's Narrative so far that helps us evaluate whether *denominations* are necessary and healthy for the Church today? Can you picture some ways that, unlike Paul, a church planting team today - even in an area not previously impacted by the Church - might have to consider the issue of denominationalism?

2. In your own words describe what is meant by "baptism of the Spirit" in the New Testament. As you consider the Narrative, particularly what Luke is describing in Acts, explain why you believe God sometimes gave amazing signs when certain groups were *baptized in the Spirit*. Should we; (a) always, (b) sometimes, or (c) never, expect to see similar signs today?

3. Trying to draw from the Narrative so far, reflect on what you feel were probably the main motivations that Paul drew on for the blend of physical, emotional, mental and spiritual discipline needed for him to keep going, year after year. Do you think his lifestyle was 'over the top' or obsessive? Do you think such a lifestyle would be excessive for someone else… for you?

→ ACTIVITIES

1. Do some online research (beyond Wikipedia) and in about half a page:

   a) Summarize the contemporary debate about *Insider Movements*.

   b) Share any thoughts you have on this issue in light of what we have covered in the Acts account so far.

2.24 God is with Paul as he ministers in Ephesus, Macedonia & Corinth

 OBJECTIVES OF THIS TUTORIAL

In this part of the Narrative, God gives Paul the ability to perform miracles to validate his ministry. The Ephesian believers recognize the contradictions between their lifestyle and what they say they believe. Paul's ministry directly causes a riot in Ephesus. He leaves Ephesus, goes to Troas, then visits churches in Macedonia and finally travels to Corinth. A plot to kill him forces him to travel to Syria. Knowing he'd probably not be back again, Paul says emotional farewells in Troas and to the Ephesian elders in Miletus. The portion of Scripture referred to in this tutorial is: **Acts 19:11-21:14**

Last time

After a time in Syrian Antioch, Paul set out on his third major church planting and establishing trip. After traveling across country he eventually arrived in Ephesus. There he found a handful of people who believed that Jesus is the Messiah. After he filled in some areas of truth for them that they were missing, they were baptized and God's Spirit demonstrated His permanent presence with them through miraculous signs. When Paul's teaching was rejected by the majority in the synagogue, he and the believers left and began to establish a separate identity as a local church. Paul stayed in Ephesus for at least two more years, teaching truth with widespread results through the entire region.

God demonstrates His power

During this time of significant expansion for the Church into these predominantly non-Jewish ethnic communities in the area known as *Asia*, God is giving special abilities to His chosen representative, Paul, to validate his teaching (Acts 19:11-20). In some amazing demonstrations of God's power - unrivalled since Jesus' years of ministry and perhaps immediately after Pentecost in Jerusalem - Paul is able to heal people of sickness just by touching them or even by them touching something he's had physical contact with.

But as has been the case right down to our times, there are people who want power without the cost of being true disciples, who are glad to use the name of Jesus for their own gain, but without ever submitting in faith to His claims. Luke records an incident that happens to some Jewish men - seven brothers in fact - that are like that. Apparently they make a living by traveling around offering to exorcise evil spirits for a fee, no doubt preying on people's gullibility. Having seen or heard about the power Paul has been given, they decide to use the name of Jesus in an incantation. But the idea backfires on them when the evil spirit who they are trying to command recognizes that, unlike Jesus and Paul, these imposters have no authority from God. He uses the man he's controlling to attack the would-be exorcists "with such violence that they fled from the house, naked and battered" Luke says.

Whether or not this episode seems bizarre or even humorous to us - with our scientific and rationalistic 21st century worldview - it certainly isn't humorous to the residents of Ephesus in the 1st century. For them, as for many people from other cultures today, trying to manipulate the spiritual world through incantations, rituals, and magic charms is a normal part of life. Even the believers, who've been born again and have God's Spirit living in them, have not up to this point understood how much they've been living according to the assumptions of their society's worldview that is dominated by Satan's deception. In many ways, their lifestyles have been a blend of the beliefs and values of their new faith, with the norms of their community. But God, who is always faithfully revealing truth to His children, now uses this incident to help the Ephesian believers clearly recognize what they've been doing. They publicly acknowledge certain evil practices and burn their incantation books that in their community are considered extremely valuable. There is no suggestion here of them needing to destroy something because of any innate evil power, but only that they are publicly and finally rejecting a system that is at odds with them trusting in God as their Father, the Son as their Saviour, and the Spirit as their Guide.

The magic books are just one of the numerous ways that Satan has devised for reinforcing the false narratives that human beings choose to believe, instead of allowing God to reveal Himself and His intentions to them. The account doesn't say, but it's possible the believers face ridicule and even harassment from their families and society for no longer participating in activities that are supposed to maintain harmony and protect everyone against harm. Whether or not they do pay this personal price on top of the financial loss, God certainly used these and similar circumstances to help drive the outward push of the Good News in the area.

Paul sends two young co-workers ahead
Luke records (Acts 19:21,22) that Paul is really wanting to go to Rome, which is about 1,300 kilometers to the west of where he is currently, in Ephesus… but first he has to go

back to Jerusalem, 1000 kilometers to the east. But before any of that, he's conscious of the need to visit the churches in Philippi, Thessalonica and others in Macedonia, and also those in Achaia province, primarily Corinth. There are certainly some problems in the Corinthian church that Paul addresses in a long letter or *epistle* that he writes from Ephesus. Luke lets us know that Timothy, the young disciple from Derbe who'd been on the last trip, and another guy called *Erastus* have both been working with Paul in Asia. Although the Apostle is obviously a strong individual, we see very few instances when he's not working with others who have the same objectives. He is always looking for opportunities to entrust responsibilities to others who share the burden of the Gospel and the care of the churches. So now, he sends his two younger co-workers, Timothy and Erastus, ahead to Macedonia while he finishes up some things in Asia.

Resentful shrine makers cause a riot in Ephesus

The Message Paul and others have been teaching has made significant inroads in the society, even impacting the local economy (Acts 19:23-40). For years, money has flowed into Ephesus from pilgrims coming to the celebrated temple of *Artemis*, who's widely worshiped as mother goddess of the earth. Many buy miniature shrines, usually tiny replicas of the temple made from silver, stone or clay, to take home or to bury in graves with their dead. But lately the craftsmen and merchants who profit most from this religious trade have noticed that sales have been dropping off sharply. A meeting is organized and angry speeches are made. "It's that Paul…telling people that handmade gods aren't gods at all. We'll be ruined. Artemis will lose her prestige." Their agitation flares into a riot that spreads through the city. People rush to the amphitheatre, many not knowing why. Unable to locate Paul, they grab his co-workers. He's keen to go and address the angry crowd but other friends, some of them government officials, talk him out of it. After some hours, calm is eventually restored to the city.

In one form or another, on large and small scales, this kind of scenario often plays out when the Gospel begins to significantly impact a community. The long-standing systems through which people seek and maintain power, prestige and profit, are often threatened by a Message that challenges the prevailing worldview, with its associated beliefs, values and behavior. Like Paul, other church planters often have to face this reality, knowing that how they respond to those who are threatened by them and their message has significant implications, not only for their own work, but also for any new church that is looking to them as a model. Where possible, it is important that they pursue relationships with people from all the levels in the society, as Paul clearly did. If the Gospel or the Church is seen as being only for one part of the society, then unnecessary divisions are being created and weaknesses built in. But as Jesus explained (Matthew 10:34-36), His exclusive claims implicit in the Gospel are hardly likely to bring harmony in relationships, communities and a world system that is dominated by rival claims. So, as His witnesses, although we should do everything to avoid being the source of offence or tensions, we have to realize that we'll often be seen as a threat to those with the most invested in the existing system, particularly when we teach truth clearly.

Paul visits churches in Macedonia and Achaia

Paul is finally ready to leave Ephesus (Acts 20:1-6). He heads north up the Aegean coast to Troas where he hopes to catch up with Titus. Although not mentioned by name in the Acts account, Paul will later refer to this Gentile believer as a trusted co-worker and will write him the short letter that we know from the New Testament by his name. Apparently Titus has recently been working in the church in Corinth, possibly after he went there from Ephesus, with Paul's letter that we know as First Corinthians. Now Paul is hoping to catch up with Titus on his return journey so he can find out how things are going in Corinth. Not finding him in Troas, he continues on across to Macedonia - where they do eventually meet up. After getting a somewhat encouraging report, Paul writes another letter - which we call Second Corinthians - that he probably asks Titus to deliver in person. Most of these details are not included in the Acts account but emerge from the content of the letters themselves.

Luke doesn't say how long Paul spends visiting the Macedonian churches like Philippi and Thessalonica but it could be as much as a year before he finally makes it down to Corinth for a few months. It's during this time that Paul writes his famous letter to the believers in Rome, and possibly the one to the Galatians that we have available in the New Testament. From the southern Greek province of Achaia he plans to sail to Syria along with many other Jews who'd typically be heading to Jerusalem for Passover at this time each year. But when he finds out there's a plan to kill him on board, he has to change his plans. Instead, he and his group of companions, who are taking a gift from the Gentile churches to the Judean believers, have to travel up around the Aegean coast into Macedonia. Eventually Paul is able to board a ship in Philippi. It seems as though doctor Luke might have been there working in the church since it was planted when he came there with Paul, Silas and Timothy a few years ago. Certainly that was the last time he was narrating the story as part of Paul's team, which he now begins to do again.

Paul visits Troas then meets the Ephesian elders

Leaving Philippi they sail around past the narrow strait known as the *Bosphorus*, famous as the place where the continents of Europe and Asia almost touch. They land in Troas where, Luke says, they "gathered with the local believers to share in the Lord's Supper" (Acts 20:7-38). It seems that this was something the early believers regularly did as part of the goodbyes when someone was leaving for a long time… perhaps echoing the sentiment of the final, farewell meal the Lord Jesus had with His disciples before His death. Paul speaks for so long that a young man sitting on a windowsill goes to sleep around midnight and falls to his death, but through God's power Paul is able to restore his life.

They continue their voyage, probably on coastal trading ships, hopping from port to port down the western coast of Asia. As part of the group now, Luke is able to give a detailed travelogue. Paul is hurrying to get to Jerusalem in time for the Festival of Pentecost and so decides not to spend time in Ephesus even though they pass by quite close. But when they land in Miletus, a port further down the coast, Paul sends a message asking the elders at the church in Ephesus to come and meet with him there. Although the two cities are only about 60 kilometers apart in a straight line, because of the geography, for them it probably means a rather difficult two-day journey. But these leaders gladly make the effort to see, for one last time, this man who first brought them the Gospel, taught them as young believers, and then discipled them as they took on their leadership responsibilities in the church.

Paul's farewell address to these men is both moving and rich with potential insights as we see the things he reminds them of from his own example, and the final exhortations he leaves with them as they care for the church he has invested so much in. He says that they have seen the humility, passion, self-sacrifice, and commitment to clarity in the Gospel that has underpinned his ministry among them. He has done everything he possibly can and fulfilled his responsibility, and now they are to do the same. Like shepherds entrusted with God's precious, blood-bought sheep, they are to watch over the believers. And to feed them with the truth while vigilantly protecting them from false teaching that will inevitably threaten. There will be hard work and sacrifice involved, but as Jesus stated, those who choose to *give* end up with more than those who just want to *take*.

Paul and friends arrive in Tyre

After an emotional and tearful goodbye they see him on to the ship. Luke carefully documents their progress towards Syria (Acts 21:1-14). One landfall they make at the eastern end of the Mediterranean is the port of Tyre, very close to today's Israel-Lebanon border. In both Tyre and Caesarea, Jerusalem believers with the gift of prophecy predict that Paul will be arrested if he goes to Jerusalem… everyone urges him not to go. But he declares that he is "ready not only to be jailed at Jerusalem but even die for the sake of the Lord Jesus" (Acts 21:13).

GOD IS WITH PAUL AS HE MINISTERS IN EPHESUS, MACEDONIA & CORINTH

? DISCUSSION POINTS

1. Although Christians in our culture are unlikely to have books of incantations on their shelves or in their e-readers, can you suggest other things (tangible or not) that we continue to rely on despite saying that we depend fully on God? If not with a bonfire, then what do you think might be our starting point for dealing with those things?

2. Describe what you think the battle with Satan and his power looks like for us today. Do you feel it is substantially very different here in our society than in other places that are less culturally 'Christian'? Please explain.

3. Can you picture yourself being part of an effort to plant a church in an area like Ephesus where the Gospel has not previously been accessible to the community? If *not*, can you reflect on the reasons. If so, put in your own words what would you like to be able to say to your friends there if you were leaving for the last time.

➡ ACTIVITIES

1. Study maps of the Mediterranean around the time of the Acts Narrative until you're able to correctly identify most of these places on the following map; Antioch in Syria, Tarsus, Damascus, Corinth, Ephesus, Thessalonica, Philippi, Athens, Colossae, Iconium and Troas.

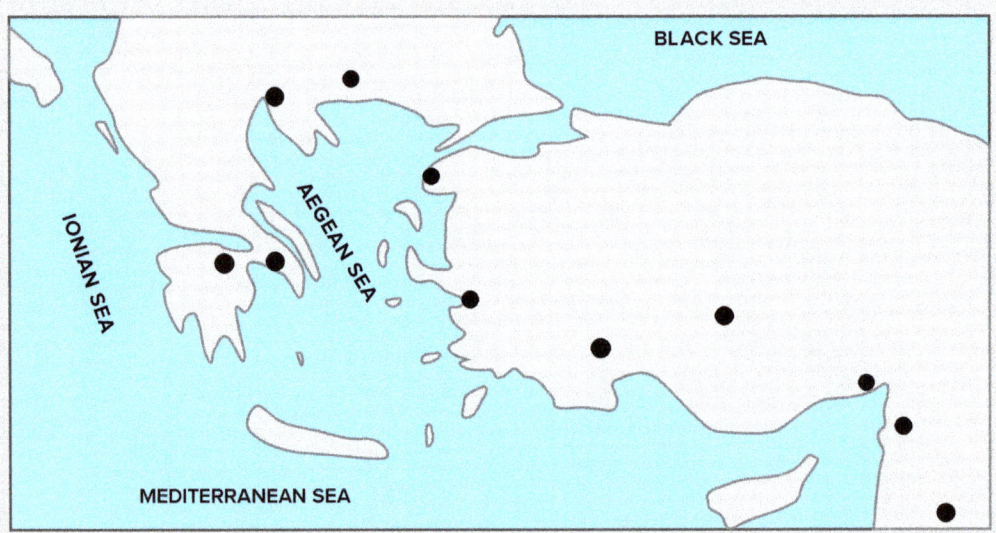

2.25 Paul is arrested in Jerusalem and imprisoned

 OBJECTIVES OF THIS TUTORIAL

In Jerusalem, Paul faces an angry mob that accuses him of religious sedition and tries to kill him. The Roman army commander arranges a meeting between Paul and the Supreme Jewish Council but it disintegrates into chaos. The Lord speaks to him, bringing reassurance and comfort. Paul is taken to Caesarea and is tried by the Roman governor. No clear verdict is reached and he is jailed, although well treated, for two years.
The portion of Scripture referred to in this tutorial is: Acts 21:15-24:27

Last time
God gave Paul the ability to perform miracles to validate his ministry. A widely reported incident involving an evil spirit caused the Ephesian believers to recognize the contradictions between their lifestyle and what they said they believed - in response they publicly burned books of incantations. A riot erupted in Ephesus when Paul's ministry seriously impacted the profits of the artisans making miniature shrines to the goddess Artemis. After leaving Ephesus, Paul went to Troas, and then visited the churches in Macedonia before making it down to Corinth. A plot to kill him forced he and his friends to travel by a circuitous route to Syria. Knowing he'd probably not be back again, Paul said emotional farewells in Troas and to the Ephesian elders in Miletus.

Paul complies with a request from Jerusalem
Luke continues his account with their arrival in Jerusalem, where they are warmly welcomed by their brothers and sisters in the faith (Acts 21:15-26). In a meeting with the leaders of the Jerusalem church, Paul has opportunity to "give a detailed account of the things God had accomplished among the Gentiles through his ministry." It is no doubt encouraging for Paul to hear the leaders praise God for the report from his ministry, but as equally disappointing when the focus immediately shifts to their local concerns and internal church politics.

This highlights the challenges that very often exist in the relationship of 'those who send and stay' with 'those who are sent and go'. Each has their own most recent experiences, focus and concerns and it can be difficult for those coming back to find that everyone at home isn't able to fully relate to the challenges, and lows and highs they've experienced 'out there'. On the other side, those in the sending church can find that their returning friends have been changed by their unique experiences, and no longer seem as interested in what's happening 'back here'. These are not insurmountable challenges, but there needs to be a real commitment on each part to really listen and try to understand.

What the Jerusalem leaders raise with Paul relates to a controversial issue that has dogged the Church since the very beginning. Almost all Jewish converts to Christianity up to this point have continued in their commitment to the Old Covenant Law. Now, however, rumors are circulating that not only does Paul tell Gentile believers that it's not necessary for them to follow Moses' law, but that he's also urging Jewish believers in other areas to abandon it, not even to circumcise their sons. So the Jerusalem elders want Paul to quell these rumors through a display of orthodoxy by joining some other men in a purification ceremony and paying for their expenses. Whatever Paul's feelings, he complies without protest and goes along to the Temple each day.

Paul is rescued from an angry mob

It's nearly the end of the seven-day ritual purification when things suddenly erupt (Acts 21:26 - 22:23). Some Jews from Asia, no doubt having stayed on after Passover, recognize Paul: "Hey it's that guy, he goes everywhere teaching against the Law… yeah, and the Temple. Brings filthy Gentiles in here. Grab him. Help, everyone. Death to Gentiles who come in here. Death to anyone bringing them in!" People come streaming from everywhere, drag Paul outside the Temple, everyone trying to land a hit or kick, they want blood… just like with Stephen years ago when Paul was an approving bystander. Word reaches the Roman commander in the nearby garrison: "Sir, it's gone crazy out there, Jews rioting about something." "Right, you there, I want two brigades. Follow me, now! On the double." The crowd parts in front of them, the ones beating Paul stop. "What's going on? Who's that you've got?" But it's no good. Everyone starts yelling, screaming accusations. "Okay, arrest him. We'll sort this out later in the fortress. Must be that terrorist leader from Egypt. You've chained his hands? Right, march. Look out, look out; they're trying to get him. Hold him up on your shoulders." They elbow roughly through the crowd that's chanting "Kill him, kill him!"

Now, up ahead on the steps to the barracks, the crowd can see the man at the center of all this controversy talking to the Roman commander. He looks surprised, but nods his head, gives a command. The soldiers turn and put the man down, stand close, guarding him. He's got his hand up. "Hey everyone, be quiet! Listen to what he has to say." What's his name, Saul or Paul, isn't it? He's speaking in good Aramaic, perfect accent. He calls them brothers and fathers. Reminds them that he's from a good Jewish family, well educated, orthodox, zealous. Yes, of course, he was a leader in the violent clampdown against the Way back when it was still new. Now he reckons he had a supernatural encounter on the road to Damascus, with Jesus from Nazareth. But he was crucified! How could that be? Who knows, maybe it *was* a vision from God of some sort? Afterwards, he says, he badly wanted to share this message with his own people. Well of course, who else would he go to? What's that? What's that? God told him no one would listen, and so he was to take this revelation to the Gentile dogs? Blasphemy! We were right. He has to die. "Kill him, kill him!"

Paul identifies himself as Roman and as a Pharisee

The commander has had enough. "Take him in and beat the truth out of him. I'll get to the bottom of this." But just as they're getting ready to whip Paul, the situation changes dramatically when Paul reveals that he's a Roman citizen. Even to shackle a Roman citizen without a conviction or charge is considered a crime - to whip one is unthinkable. The next day the commander takes a different approach (Acts 22:24-23:9).

The 71 Jewish religious leaders - the Council, or *Sanhedrin* - are summoned to a meeting, and Paul is made to stand in front of them. During the following exchanges, Luke records three times that Paul addresses these men as "brothers". The third time is when he identifies himself as a second generation Pharisee, asserting that he's on trial for believing that people will rise from the dead. He does this knowing that the Council is divided between Pharisees and Sadducees and that the flashpoint of controversy between the two leading Jewish sects is resurrection.

It is very instructive to note Paul's nuanced sense of his own identity and how he wisely highlights different aspects of who he is, depending on the context and the purpose of a particular interaction. Clearly Paul sees himself first and foremost as a *disciple* and *witness* of the Lord Jesus. Then, in most of his letters that we have, he opens by stating that he's an *Apostle*, primarily to the Gentiles. He serves as one of God's designated Storytellers - a *prophet*...he's also a *church builder*, a spiritual *father* to many, and a *brother*. Without any sense of contradiction, he's also a *tent-maker*, someone who works with his hands. When necessary, he'll highlight his impeccable *Jewish credentials*, and at other times assert his legal rights as a *Roman citizen*. If needed, he cites *educational qualifications* and claims his *hometown status*. With Jewish leaders he's a *Pharisee* and *son of a Pharisee*; with Gentile believers he plays down his Jewishness; for the sake of the legalist Judean Christians he'll go through an orthodox purification ceremony. He speaks perfect Aramaic or Hebrew to Jews and fluent Greek to a Roman commander. There's no lack of integrity in presenting himself in these different ways, they are all perfectly real and valid. Nor is this about protecting or promoting himself...instead, it is all about being *who he needs to be* to help others know the One with whom Paul identifies so closely.

Jesus encourages Paul to stand strong

With the argument between the Pharisees and Sadducees on the Council quickly headed for a brawl, Paul has to again be rescued by the Roman soldiers (Acts 23:10,11). Held in the barracks for a couple more days, Paul is perhaps wrestling with uncertainties about where all this is headed. How does this serve the Lord's purposes? But in the night he sees Jesus standing right there, encouraging him to be brave. "Paul, this is all about you being able to tell people about me here in Jerusalem and in Rome." Any frustration or fear must have immediately been replaced by a sense of peace and quiet joy. Perhaps lying in the dark cell he remembers things he'd been trying to say to the believers in Rome facing similar difficulties… for us who love God and have been invited to be involved in His purposes, every circumstance works out for our good (Romans 8:28).

Paul is taken to be tried by the governor

Certainly the encouragement from the Lord is timely. Paul is in real danger and this ordeal has only just begun (Acts 23:12-24:27). At the same time, if he's prepared, there will also be great opportunities to share truth with people who might otherwise never have a chance to hear. The Commander of the Roman forces in Jerusalem decides to get Paul out of the city and down to Caesarea. Through a nephew of Paul, a plot to kill the Apostle by Jewish zealots has been uncovered. In the Roman provincial capital there'll be better prison facilities away from the immediate reach of the Jewish leaders. That night a large force of infantry and cavalry escorts Paul to the halfway point, and other mounted troops take him the rest of the 100 kilometers to the coast.

Five days later the High Priest with some of his colleagues and a Jewish lawyer come to argue their case against Paul before Felix, the Roman governor of Judea (fifth or sixth in line since Pontius Pilate). They accuse him of being a ringleader of the subversive cult that reveres Jesus of Nazareth, and of profaning the Jewish Temple, something certain to bring strife in this volatile Roman province. Paul has an opportunity to respond, and explains that there is no evidence for the charges against him. It turns out that the governor is quite familiar with *the Way* - a term Luke uses regularly for early Christianity in his Narrative. He adjourns the hearing without any definite verdict, but he is at least sympathetic enough to allow Paul some freedom and visiting rights. A few days later, Felix brings his Jewish wife to also hear Paul speak about faith in Jesus the Messiah, but the governor cuts him off when the conversation turns to God's view of behavior that falls short of His perfect standards. Luke comments that over the coming months Felix talks to Paul quite often, but he leaves him in jail for two years hoping to be paid a bribe for his release.

? DISCUSSION POINTS

1. The Holy Spirit rarely led Luke to pass any comment on the choices the key characters like Paul made in the events he records. But what do you think about Paul's decision to comply with the Jerusalem elders' request for him to take part in the purification ceremony at the Temple? Does this seem to line up with, or violate, what we've seen so far of Paul's teaching and previous actions? Please explain.

2. Reflect on the way Paul highlighted different aspects of his identity in different settings. Can you give an example of how you might apply this principle without jeopardizing your integrity (a) here in your own society, and (b) in a country that legally restricts teaching God's Word?

3. Imagine that you've been sharing God's Narrative up to this point with a friend who is then put in jail for sharing his or her faith. Now after two years you have opportunity to smuggle in a brief message to them. What would you write to help them be patient and not despair?

2.26 Paul is taken to Rome and teaches there for two years

 OBJECTIVES OF THIS TUTORIAL

Paul is given a trial before the governor in Caesarea, but denies he has committed any crime and asks to be brought before Caesar in Rome. He has a chance to speak to King Agrippa and his sister before beginning the long and eventful journey to Rome. Paul remains under house arrest for two years, but is able to teach and write letters to the churches.

The portion of Scripture referred to in this tutorial is: **Acts 24:27-28:31**

Last time

In Jerusalem, Paul complied with a request of the church leaders that he participate in a Jewish ritual purification to demonstrate his orthodoxy. At the temple he had to be rescued by Roman soldiers when an angry mob accused him of religious sedition and tried to kill him. The Roman army commander arranged a meeting between Paul and the Supreme Jewish Council but it disintegrated into chaos. At night the Lord spoke to him, bringing reassurance and comfort. With Paul's life under threat the commander had him taken to Caesarea, where he was tried by the Roman governor. No clear verdict was reached and he was jailed, although well treated, for two years.

Paul uses his right as to "appeal to Caesar"

Eventually the governor, Felix - known by history for his brutality and corruption - is replaced by Porcius Festus who will die after only two years in this appointment. Soon after his arrival he makes the trip from the coast up to Jerusalem, where the religious leaders waste no time in putting their case against Paul to the new Roman ruler (Acts 24:27-25:12). They want him brought up to Jerusalem for trial, secretly hoping to have him ambushed and killed on the way. But Festus says he'll try the case in Caesarea, so the leaders go there soon after and make their accusations against Paul in court. When Paul denies having committed any crime, Festus - no doubt eager to make a good early impression in this province that's notoriously difficult to govern - asks him if he's willing to stand trial in Jerusalem. But Paul realizes by now he won't get justice from Festus, he is aware of the Jewish leaders' evil intent and, most importantly, he's determined to get to Rome and do whatever God has for him there, even if it means going as a prisoner. So in a move that effectively takes the matter out of the governor's jurisdiction, he formally *appeals to Caesar*... in other words, he claims his right as a Roman citizen to be tried by the imperial court in Rome.

Paul has opportunity to speak before King Agrippa

The governor Festus knows that he has no choice (Acts 25:13-26:32); he'll have to send Paul to be tried by the emperor. But it's a most unusual case. There's no evidence of any Roman laws being broken by this Roman citizen, and yet there's a widespread demand for the death sentence for the former Pharisee allegedly violating the laws of his own people. What is the governor to say in the written explanation of the case that will accompany the prisoner to Rome? An opportunity for some advice comes with the visit of King Agrippa, great-grandson of Herod the Great, and his sister Bernice. Curious to hear this former Pharisee who's willing to risk everything for the sake of "a dead man named Jesus" he insists is actually alive, Agrippa and his sister come back the next day.

So Paul has the opportunity to tell his story once again before this quasi-Jewish ruler who grew up in Rome under the patronage of the Emperor Claudius. It's noticeable that Paul makes adjustments in order to connect and communicate with his audience. This time it's his own Jewishness rather than his Roman citizenship that he stresses in describing his initial persecution of the believers, then his dramatic conversion and commissioning by the resurrected Jesus. He concludes with an appeal to Agrippa's knowledge of the prophets and tries to convince him that everything they said has been fulfilled in the life, death and resurrection of Jesus of Nazareth. One thing Paul doesn't mention in his address is how years ago in Damascus, when Jesus stated that He'd chosen him to take His message to the surrounding ethnic groups as well as to the Jews, He also said that Paul would share the truth with kings.

In the intervening years since that first encounter, if he'd pictured the Lord's words coming true, it's likely that being a prisoner wasn't part of the dream. But by now, Paul has been through so much in his journey with his Master, that he is not even craving a prominent or glorious role in the unfolding Narrative...for him the important thing is that Jesus is seen and known by people. Being full or hungry, respected or humiliated, at peace or under stress, free or locked up... those things have become increasingly less important. He knows that it's not even his story anyway, but he's just glad to have a part if he is bringing glory to God and contributing somehow to His amazing purposes. As the royal party in Caesarea leave the hall where they've heard Paul's story, they agree that he has committed no crime, but he has appealed to Caesar, and so to Rome he must go.

Paul and the others begin the long trek to Rome

Along with some other prisoners being taken to Italy, the Apostle is placed in the custody of an officer, a commander of the Augustan or Imperial Regiment that has been serving in Syria (Acts 27:1-5). He and his soldiers will accompany Paul on what will prove to be an eventful trip, to say the least. The first ship they board is from near Troas, on the Aegean… a coastal trader that is probably heading home carrying cargo and passengers for different stops along the way. Doctor Luke has obviously decided to go with Paul to Rome because he narrates the rest of this story as an eyewitness. In fact, he has almost certainly been with Paul since they arrived here two years ago. It has been suggested that Luke probably stayed in Caesarea to be a support for Paul, and that it is during this time he collected eyewitness accounts from the disciples and others that he'd later compile, under the Spirit's guidance, as his *Gospel*. Another friend of theirs from Macedonia, Aristarchus, had come with them to Jerusalem and now he continues to travel with them, possibly as a personal assistant to Paul.

They head up the coast and dock at Sidon, a port about 40 kilometers south of modern day Beirut. The commander Julius is kind to Paul and lets him visit some friends there. The next day, as they head out they strike the first hint of the problems that lie ahead. Their course lies to the northwest but by now it's autumn and the *etesians* - strong, dry winds - are blowing from that direction, as they do most years. The square sailed ships of the time are not well suited to heading 'close to the wind' and so they are struggling, even to make it across the corner of the Mediterranean to the coast of Asia. Instead of going the straightest route, they have to loop up around the top end of Cyprus and parallel the coast until, around two weeks later, they land at Myra, on the southwest tip of Asia Minor.

They make it to Crete against contrary winds

The commander finds another ship that's headed their direction (Acts 27:6-12). Larger than the coastal trader they've been on, this one is a grain ship, sailing between Alexandria in Egypt and Italy. They've come across to Myra first before making the long haul west into the teeth of the dangerous autumn weather. They set out, full of grain and nearly 300 passengers… progress is slow. They sail on the eastern side of the island of Crete to get what protection they can from the wind that is howling now from the northwest. It takes another couple of weeks of tedious tacking back and forth to make their next port, an open bay, about a third of the way along the 260 kilometer long island. There's no mention of a vision from God, but somehow Paul senses trouble ahead. He speaks up but the commander, the captain and ship owner are keen to push on for Italy and don't listen to his warning.

After two weeks in a storm they are shipwrecked

At first things seem okay, but then the wind changes and suddenly they're being battered by gale-force winds from the northeast that all sailors in the Mediterranean know and fear. They're being blown further south and even though it's still 600 kilometers away, they worry they'll be driven onto the desolate stretch of sand banks off the north coast of Libya (Acts 27:13-44).

This is only the start of their ordeal. One terrifying day blends into the next until it seems like this nightmare will never end. Some of the wheat cargo has been thrown over and even the ship's tackle, to lighten the ship. No one is even bothering to eat any more. No doubt the soldiers and crew ask for the help of every deity they have ever heard of, but all to no avail... they've given up all hope. But of course Paul knows of a different reality, and he takes the opportunity to share this with them. Unlike their voiceless false gods, the true God that he belongs to and serves has communicated with him. This Creator God is not a helpless victim of natural forces - His intentions, like sending Paul to stand before the Emperor of Rome, won't flounder even in the face of the worst storm. Not only is He powerful, but He's merciful as well... He's going to rescue everyone on the ship even though they don't know Him. They'll be shipwrecked on an island, but they'll all survive.

And that's exactly what happens. They've battled the storm for two weeks and drifted 750 kilometers through open ocean when, in the middle of the night, the experienced sailors sense that they are close to land. As dawn breaks they are able to make out a small bay with a beach in an unfamiliar coast. They raise a sail and head towards it but before they can make it in through the breakers they run aground on a sand bank. With the waves smashing the boat to pieces around them, everyone jumps into the ocean and eventually makes it to shore, either swimming or holding on to planks.

Three months in Malta and then off to Italy

The sailors, soldiers, prisoners and passengers from the ship find out from people on the beach that they are on the island of Malta (Acts 28:1-14). They are treated kindly by the locals and by the Roman official stationed there. God demonstrates His power before the islanders when Paul is unaffected by the bite of a poisonous snake and when Paul (and possibly Luke) is used to heal a number of sick people. They are shown respect and gratitude and when the time comes for them to leave they are given everything they need for their onward journey. There is no mention of conversions or a church being planted then, perhaps a language barrier made real communication of truth impossible. There is, however, a tradition in Malta that it was through the Apostle Paul the Gospel first came to their island, but there's no real way to know for sure if this is factual or not.

After three months, spring brings more favorable weather and passage is found for them on another grain ship from Egypt that has wintered on the island. After leaving Malta, they head north to Syracuse on the eastern coast of the island of Sicily, then to Rhegium on the toe of Italy. Finally, they sail up the coast and into the bay of Naples with the active volcano Vesuvius looming overhead. Only 19 years after Paul's arrival it will erupt and famously bury the town of Pompeii at its base. They land in Puteoli, site of modern day Pozzuoli, the nearest harbor to the city of Rome and a hub of commercial and naval shipping for the Empire.

Paul lives under house arrest in Rome

They still have a land journey of about 240 kilometers ahead of them, so after being allowed to spend a week with a group of believers at the coastal city, they make their way to the *Via Apia* or *Appian Way* and then follow it towards the capital (Acts 28:15-31). The believers in Rome have found out that Paul and friends are coming, and they come to meet them on the road... some even traveling over 60 kilometers to welcome the Apostle. They haven't met him in person before, but of course they know him through the wonderful letter he wrote to them some 5 years ago. This is, of course, a huge encouragement to Paul, who has finally made it to the capital of the Empire, although not in the way he perhaps originally intended.

Although Paul is under guard all the time, because he hasn't committed a serious crime, and isn't considered a political threat, he's allowed to live in a house in the city that he rents himself, and he's free to invite people to visit. It seems that Luke stays with him in Rome for some time because later, in letters to the fellowship in Colossae and to a leader from that church, Philemon, the Apostle sends greetings from Doctor Luke. During this period of incarceration Paul will also write letters or epistles to the churches in Ephesus and Philippi. Soon after arriving in Rome, Paul has opportunity to share the truth about Jesus the Messiah with local Jewish leaders. It is clear that he is not bitter towards his own Jewish people, even though they have treated him so badly and tried to kill him just two years ago in Jerusalem. As has been the case throughout the entire Acts account, the response of these Jews in Rome to the Good News is mixed - some are persuaded but others refuse to believe.

Luke concludes his book about the amazing things Jesus has accomplished through His Apostles since His return to His Father, by briefly describing Paul's ministry in Rome. For two years he has opportunity to speak openly about God's sovereign purposes on earth that He has made possible through the Lord Jesus Christ. At the very beginning of Luke's account, he recorded the command of Jesus to His disciples that they should go out as His witnesses to the ends of the earth. In the three decades that are described in his book, through their efforts the *Ecclesia* has spread from its small beginnings in

PAUL IS TAKEN TO ROME AND TEACHES THERE FOR TWO YEARS

Jerusalem out through the Roman world and beyond. As His Body in *this* generation we are called, like Peter, Philip, Stephen, James and Paul, to continue taking His Message out to the communities and ethnic groups everywhere that, after 2000 years, are still without access to the Good News.

❓ DISCUSSION POINTS

1. Imagine you've shared this much of God's Narrative with someone and seen them come to faith... they are here studying in university but will soon return to their home country where sharing Christian teaching is illegal, often resulting in persecution and long prison sentences. How would you advise them? What sections and/or themes would you highlight from the Acts account?

2. As we view the life of Paul, one thing that stands out is his unwavering sense of confidence in the overall direction and purpose for his life. Can you name three to five key things that, at this stage in your life, serve as guides or touchstones or 'core values' that underpin your priorities and decisions? If not, can you reflect on why this is and perhaps describe your search for this kind of definition?

3. Please feel free to share anything, either general or specific, that stands out as you reflect back on this study of the Acts Narrative.

➡ ACTIVITIES

1. Do any research necessary so that you know who *King Agrippa* was and a little about his (and the other Herods') relationship to the Jews and Judaism.

2. Re-read Paul's address to Agrippa and his sister Bernice in Acts 26. Note down any instances of Paul *contextualizing* in order to communicate truth with them.

ACCESSTRUTH

Training Resources for Making Truth *Accessible*.

RESOURCES FOR

> Discipleship
> Evangelism
> Church Planting
> Language Learning
> Bible Translation
> Cross-cultural work

Equipping God's people to be more effective as they serve in cross-cultural contexts, either locally or globally.